Playdates with the Divine

Lisa M. Smith, Ph.D.

The Divine sleeps in the stories,

Dreams in the plants,

Stirs in the animals,

Awakens in humanity

And plays in us all.

Original Play, Anonymous

To the amazing women in my life who continually

inspire me with their stories.

I am blessed to have so many beautiful, strong women I call friends!

Here's to strong women -

May we know them -

May we raise them -

May we **be** them!

My Dearest New Playmate:

I have had many questions about the Divine in my life. I have meandered down many paths to answer these questions. Some paths I willingly embarked on. Others, well, let's just say I felt *shoved* onto those paths. I have also sought answers by way of others - through *their* teachings, lives, words, and books. Although many of these teachers provided great insight and inspiration, they could never really answer *my* particular questions about the Divine. Some of them could not answer their own questions. They simply covered up the questions with "dogmas" and "shoulds" or "God says ___," while others truly *had* answered their own questions, only to find they revealed more questions, so they began pursuing those.

I found that the answers themselves weren't what I was seeking, after all. I was learning to *live* the questions themselves, as the questions brought me to this divine and sacred presence. In doing this, I began wrestling with the "name" I called this presence. Although God had resonated with me (and still does), I found the name brought up a lot of fragmented energy. I found the perfect name, "Divine", as this captured how I felt when enveloped in this sacred, unconditionally loving presence.

I never had to search for it… I still don't even know how to *find* the Divine. Probably because It is not lost, or even absent, from me. However, I have learned when I am still, It finds me. I have acquired this stillness, ironically, through movement. This movement is a state of grace. I call it Play.

I love the quote "Happiness often sneaks in through a door you did not know you left open." This is how Play works. While we are letting go of the heaviness of life - the burdens and responsibilities we tend to wear like undergarments, get cast aside. Here, in all your nakedness you learn to stand unashamed, deliciously and deliriously embracing all of YOU.

I enjoy meditation and the calmness of Presence and stillness of just being. It is a great practice. I love moments of prayer – actually, I think I am in continuous communion with the Divine. It's like an unending conversation.

But, there is something about Play that tunes into some deep and rooted essence that is excavated in this moment of reckless abandon. For years, I've watched children jump into this place – in fact, for the very first years of their lives they tend to live there. They will go into the great space of "no-thingness" to play *in* nothing, *with* nothing yet create endlessly! It is magical. It is as if they have not yet learned what it is like to be "real". Ah...*that* is magic; *that* is wonderment...because to be "real" is often the opposite of that which is *really* true. We just believe it and make it so.

At first, Play is something you "do". Just like meditation, it is a practice that one takes on because it brings pleasure and relief. The more one practices play, the more one *becomes* it. Every action, word and thought becomes one of perpetual playfulness.

Innately our essence *is* play. We know this when we are children. It is love. It is the Divine coming through us. I help define "PLAy" using an acronym:

P- Perpetually
L-Laughing
A-At
y-yourself (little "y" – as this represents the ego/fear – hereafter known as Feargo ☺).

"PLAy" is not a thing to laugh at for the point of making fun. It is laughing - as in not taking everything seriously. Play is simply the opening through which the Divine drops in. It's a space that is created where anything is possible. There are no rules, boundaries or limitations. It is as if the power to create has met the space of endless possibilities. All energy is focused on opening and allowing spontaneous creation to come through. It is an in-betweeness.

And if you are very, very quiet – you can hear your own inner giggle arising somewhere from deep inside of you. As it breaks the surface, you might feel a vibratory hum that if you tune into will most likely beckon you right back into life…your life – You know the one you left on the elementary school playground.

The Tibetans have a word, "bardo", meaning "an in-between time". It would seem that in life we are always "in between" – beginning with the concept that the life we live is actually "in between" birth and death. We are "in between" wakefulness and sleeping, "in-between" hunger and eating, "in-between" talking and silence. It is actually the pause, the "in-between" the notes - the stillness, where all creation is born. Yet, for most of us, this sacred place of stillness from which we birth all things can be a very disturbing, if not downright alarmingly loud place. Michael Beckwith, in his book *Spiritual Liberation*, talks about this as the space we create that allows the Universe to be conscious of Itself through us. This space is the "in between" space. It is contacted through play.

What scares most adults about play is the fact that we have become accustomed to having rules, lists, and guidelines by which we order and measure our lives. Having a checklist and some quantifiable data gives a fabricated meaning to the things that we do. Coloring outside the lines is something we innately do as children, but quickly learn is not acceptable in our adult life. Although, interestingly enough, those that do so eventually become known as our geniuses, our shining stars – Bill Gates, Steve Jobs, Lady Gaga, etc. Why do we discourage so much individual expression and coloring outside the lines, yet envy it or celebrate it when we see it?

Because innately we know the *real* truth…that the individual expression of the Divine is truly what we are all about. We are Divine in form – expressing different aspects of creation, ingenuity and endless possibilities. We just get scared.

To play – authentically play is to live in an open-hearted, open-minded, and open-handed space. Yet to return to this space from which we naturally came into, we must traverse through many paths, accumulate knowledge, wisdom and experience. Then, in a single moment of pure joy and ecstasy, we relinquish it all just to be whatever it is that the knowledge, wisdom, and experience have carved away.

We think this life that what we accumulate throughout our journey is what makes our journey meaningful. As we traverse further along the path, we recognize it is what we give away that truly makes our lives full of love, joy and peace. Like Michelangelo, the Divine already sees the statue hidden beneath the marble. Yet it is necessary to have all that we have in order to *choose* to relinquish it. Otherwise, the trickster mind will continue to barrage us with the belief that our happiness is somehow out *there*.

The beginning of our human experience is about learning. It is necessary. We learn how to be here, in this time-space-continuum. We learn skills to help us perform tasks. There is a goal, or something to achieve. Authentic play is more about un-learning. Like a river that erodes away hard rock to create a canyon, play strips us down to the essence of who we are, less the accumulated debris from the learning our lives have given us. Much of what we learned had little or nothing to do with us. They were beliefs, thoughts and feelings of others who were passed on to us as *truth*. Whose truth?

We spend half our lives accumulating a lot of baggage, emotionally, physically, and spiritually, and then we spend the rest of our lives letting it go.

When we play we dance in a space of no-thing-ness where we can examine our *stuff*. It's a sacred, safe space where we can let go and just see who we really are. We get to dump the toy box of our lives and look at that which we no longer want to play with. Sometimes we even get to choose new toys.

The *gift* is that we become aware of our choices.

As we play with the Divine, we look deeper - beyond the surface. Fred Donaldson calls it a second look – I call it X-Ray vision. The ability to look beyond what is happening in the moment and look into its essence…the beingness – the formless that sits just beyond what is in front of you. The "never-neverland" of existence that requires just a little bit of faith, trust and yes…pixie dust…which comes in the form of letting go of all that you *think* you know about what life is. This is truly the land of magic…where anything is possible. If only you believe.

I have outlined here, what I call The ESSENCE of Play:

E – Experiential – the knowing comes from living the questions
S – Senses – going beyond what we see, touch, taste, hear, and smell
S – Spontaneous – allowing what wants to happen - happen
E – Endless, boundless Energy
N – No pre-conceived ideas…dropping into nothingness
C – Creative – natural and free-flowing
E – Expressing one's true nature

Children drop easily into their essences through play. There is no limit or an idea that must happen – just a series of strung-together, imaginative concepts that continually change and evolve. You never really know what the end game or end result will be. You just go with it, stay in the moment, and see what happens.

I noticed as my children entered school that all of a sudden, keeping score, rules and "winning" became part of play. ☹ They were learning or sadly *unlearning* how to play in the real world. That explained the little less spark in their play and spring in their steps. We adults were teaching them "how the real world works." It is unfortunate that we do not allow *them* to teach *us* how the make-believe (interesting words…MAKE BELIEVE!) world works. For in this land – anything is possible.

This book is a series of playdates with the Divine. It is where essence skipped in through a door I didn't know I had left open. Play for me, although filled with joy and exuberance, often felt less like those things in the moment, and more like an opportunity to practice what I was becoming – much like a little child playing dress-up or pretend. These experiences allowed me to wiggle around in the empty space I had created to play dress-up and really look at what was working (and not working) in my life. In this space, I got to experience the Divine in an amazing, open, unconditionally loving space. In this space, I was loved back to life.

It is my desire that your "ESSENCE" will come out and play and that you too will skip with the Divine.

I'll meet you at the swings, where we will soar to new heights!

Playfully,

Lisa

We do not stop playing because we grow old.

We grow old because we stop playing

Benjamin Franklin

Out beyond ideas of right doing and wrong doing,

there is a field.

I'll meet you there.

Rumi

Playing Pretend

How does something out there (formless) come in to right here (form)?

The Tao te Ching says, "We work with being, but non-being is what we use." It continues to say that, "Being and non-being create each other."

How does something become "real" anyway?

I think the process of the creation of life and giving birth as a great example of how something comes into being.

1) There is an idea or thought, "I want to have a baby!" which turns into a very strong desire or passion.
2) Then you must take an action to make this happen, (have sex ☺ or even better make love. Isn't it neat that the process of creation begins with a conscious intention to "make love!")?
3) You then allow the Divine to handle the details. At this point, you must let go, trust and allow.
4) Once the seed is planted, you nourish it. Notice that it remains in solitude and total darkness while it is *becoming*.
5) When it is fully grown and ready, the birthing process begins:
   a) The water breaks
   b) Labor (this involves work, sweat and tears!)
   c) Crowning
   d) Birth
   e) Afterbirth

When we look at this in terms of bringing forth an idea, or project we can envision a similar process. An idea becomes a very strong passion, which propels you to physically do something to start the ball rolling. Once you have done that, you trust in the co-creation (allow the

1

Universe to handle the details) with the Divine. Then, you nourish the seed (often-times in solitude and darkness – sharing only the details of your passion when it has passed the tricky first trimester period).

Once the birthing process begins, there can be work, difficulty (resistance, pain, issues to overcome). Then, the project crowns and is birthed into the world and what no longer serves (limited beliefs, thoughts, feelings) are released.

Meditation:

Take a deep breath. Imagine the space just behind your heart. Imagine the endless capacity there and imagine it connecting you to the Divine. Feel the all-encompassing love just beyond you. Imagine this love consuming your entire being.

Breathe this in. Allow that love to expand outward – in front of you. Imagine that this is all there is.

In This Sacred Place of Play Filled with Divine Love, Ask Yourself:

What do I want to make real in my life?

What can I let go of to make room for this?

Making Mudpies

Watch as a child with dirt and water make magic. All of a sudden with just a moment of imagination dirt and water have become exquisite mudpies - served to royalty on princess plates at a magnificent ball! Making something out of nothing and adding water and mud has never tasted so delicious!

Our innate selves know we are here to create – to mix a whole lot of things together in varying combinations to produce wonder. Life mirrors a recipe in many ways. When we first learn how to "cook" in life, we combine ingredients based on a pre-printed, relatively basic and standardized recipe. We follow it closely and typically do not vary from it when we are first learning. As we grow and change and allow the creative energy to flow within us, we begin to add a few new ingredients here and there, just, you know, to taste. Sometimes, we learn that replacing ingredients can change the dish entirely. We discover that we like certain things and that some things we used to like do not work so well anymore. Or we substitute different ingredients to make it more our own. As we continue to grow and develop, we start to completely design our own recipes - ones we create from nothing – throwing out the book altogether!

Eventually, we learn to play with the ingredients and gain a sense of confidence that allows us to throw out the measuring cups and spoons and rely on our intuitive knowing of how much. Soon, we are crackin' eggs and throwing things into a bowl with reckless abandon knowing that it might not follow a prescribed recipe – but it will all turn out right because we are finally trusting the Cook! ☺

This is what authentic play does. It holds a place where the unknown – the unborn – the not-yet-created can come forth.

Lisa M. Smith, Ph.D.

As we continue to play, adding and subtracting ingredients in life – a little more love here, a little less fear, a little more forgiveness, a little less anger – we start creating more and more of what we want and it tastes so incredibly scrumptious. Making something out of nothing *becomes* our way of being in the world. We learn to sit in the empty spaces of creation with anticipation of what is about to break forth – knowing that it always will. If we just sit, wait, watch and wonder…

The Tao te Ching states that "In doing nothing, everything is done." It can be a difficult concept to wrap our brains around simply because the idea of doing nothing is not how our human selves operate. This is not a sedentary position, however. There is a subtle different with great distinction between not doing anything and a "non-doingness." Non-doing is a very engaging and purposeful position. It is the essence of play. Where on the outside it appears as though what one is doing is "nothing" while what is happening is a stripping away of all that is unnecessary to create space from which the REAL something will come forth. A law of physics states "Nothing happens until something moves." We focus on the movement part of this…but what is really truth is the "nothing" part. Maybe it should say, "Nothing happens…Then something moves." Being able to sit with "nothing" until that which wants to come forth and move, does is essentially what play is about…stripping away, sitting in the silence and letting the Divine move in, through us and as us. Play is where this happens.

Joy does all things without concern;

For emptiness, stillness, tranquility, tastelessness,

Silence, and non-action

Are the root of all things.

Chuang Tzu

Meditation:

Breathe in peace, exhale joy. Breathe in peace, exhale joy. Breathe in peace, exhale joy. As you imagine yourself enveloped in peace, joy and enrobed in love, allow that love to overtake your breath and just breathe you!

In This Sacred Place of Play Filled with Divine Love, Ask Yourself:

How can I experience more peace in my life?

How can I experience more joy in my life?

How can I experience more love in my life?

Breathe. Listen.

Lisa M. Smith, Ph.D.

Playing With Water

There are days when things flow like water from a river, days when things gush like a geyser and then days when there seems to be a big boulder stuck in the middle of the water flow that no matter what you do, it won't budge. It seems there is a definite ebb and flow to emotions, hormones and to the general nature of life. Today I feel stuck. I have meditated, exercised, meditated more and cannot find that space that allows all things to flow. So, I decide to sit with it. Nothing is inherently wrong, but it doesn't seem as though those things are "right" either. I feel expectations about others that I normally do not feel and I feel disappointed that others are not rising to the occasion. I feel anxiety about what needs to be done, yet no real motivation to do anything about it. I feel uncertainty about a future that I felt peace and contentment with yesterday. I feel like I'm moving through mud, yet stuck in a repetitive motion that gets me nowhere. Pema Chodrin, in her book, *When Things Fall Apart*, says sometimes "Life just nails you." I have felt this – I'm not sure that's it. This just feels as though life has covered me in sticky glue and I am powerless to move. A Universal, "I've been slimed" experience!

It feels like life just sucked the play right out of me!

I understand that I have two choices. I can spin around in circles, trying to shake myself loose from this stuck-ness, or I can stay here and find a place of comfort and just *be* with the uncomfortable sticky feeling. Well, I'd like to say I always choose the latter, but usually I spend a whole lot of time doing the former, to the point of exhaustion in which the latter is a result of no more strength. But that is where I am, so it is what I do.

Now in a place of stuck uncertainty, I try to ponder my way out. Is there a magical prayer or a ritual that could hasten the passing of this

Lisa M. Smith, Ph.D.

very uncomfortable feeling? Alas, there is none. It is the integration of this oh-so-uncomfortable feeling with life…. neither thinking too much nor feeling too little about it, but allowing it to resonate in the backdrop of my life and not in the forefront. I can resume daily living knowing that this un-comfortableness will dissipate when it has had its say and that by merely nodding to it in acknowledgement of its presence, I have done enough. I pop in a silly movie, snuggle under a blanket and nourish myself. I invite Un-comfortableness to join me for a movie playdate. It nestles in beside me. We negotiate a temporary truce.

Un-comfortableness might or might not be there again when I awake in the morning. But like the cranky neighbor you have that you finally make peace with, you merely nod in acknowledgment to one another and go about your business.

This too shall pass.

Meditation:

Take a deep breath. To play is to ask questions in which there is no answer….it is the questions themselves that are to be lived and loved through…they are the keys to unlocking hidden doors within your soul. Breathe into the questions themselves, allowing the questions to be enough.

In This Sacred Place of Play Filled with Divine Love, Ask Yourself:

Can I accept the un-comfortableness for what it is?

Can I just be with it, without judgment until it passes?

Can I nourish myself through the places in me where play needs to be loved back to life?

The Splashpad

I love to write at an open mall near my home. I sit outside of my favorite little coffee place next to the splashpad. In the early morning, it is very quiet except for the splashing of the water and the wind rustling through the palm trees and the "beach-like" music playing in the background.

Then slowly, one by one, the kids come. The place begins to light up with the laughter and sheer exuberant joy that comes when children and water meet. There is no end to the screeching and gleeful dunking, splashing, running and fluid play that spontaneously erupts – over and over again. There are no electronics. They are unnecessary. The children have baptized themselves with authentic play and their essence invigorates me.

I love being near that kind of joy. It is awe-inspiring. It reminds me to play. It reminds me to "find water" – to nourish myself. It reminds me to take off my shoes and skip gleefully uninhibited into wonderment.

Do you have a splashpad?

Where can you set aside your life, kick off your shoes, let your hair down, and run with reckless abandon into sheer joy?

If you don't have one – or cannot remember, I invite you to go to a park or a place where there are children and just observe them at play. See if something in the way they move effortlessly and without any rules spurs something deep within you.

I have found that I splash the best with those who don't mind getting wet too. Sure, I can splash alone…but the collective splashing

11

becomes particularly gleeful when joined by others who enjoy kicking water around.

I watch children who don't even know each other join in their mutual adoration and worship at the watering hole. I see toys shared, playful gestures given and all parents joining in and watching out for *all* of the children. People laugh, join in conversation and the vibration in the air is sheer joy.

Life not only is delicious – it *feels* delicious in this moment!

Life is a participation sport…you do not get wet from the *word* water – you have to jump in.

Goggles anyone?

Meditation:

Take a deep breath. Imagine standing under a huge waterfall, with water cascading over you. Imagine your head turned up and your mouth opening up to drink in this delicious liquid. Feel the water running through your hands and imagine that as it washes over you it is rinsing away all of the stress and momentary disconnection-from-your-authentic-self. Imagine it filling you with peace and joy – but mostly love. Drink it in. Stay here as long as you need.

In This Sacred Place of Play Filled with Divine Love, Ask Yourself:

Can I drink in the love that is available to me right now?

Can I imagine that I am pure love – and only this?

Hide-N-Seek

I love a good game of hide-n-seek. Someone counts while everyone scatters to find that perfect space to hide. That delicious, yet slightly edgy feeling of time ticking away while scrambling to find a space to hide.

It reminds me of our spiritual journey where there is a certain hiding and seeking that takes place deep within our own being. So many talk of enlightenment. It can seem like an elusive place to seek. Others who have obtained it leave behind little clues – sort of like M&M droppings to be picked up to try to find one's way to it. Yet, it often feels to me like when I played "I spy" with a two-year-old. You are looking for something only *they* see, know, understand and that they can describe – what they see is clearly in *their* eyes only!

Personally I have experienced what I like to call *en-darkenment*. My greatest lessons have occurred as I traverse through the darkened places of my life. The Sufis say that "light" is what we know about ourselves while dark is the mysterious places in ourselves that we don't know. Dark is the "beingness" of formlessness – that which has yet to be. When it steps into the light, it becomes *form*. Much like a baby that spends 9 months in total darkness preparing to come into the light. When the light within us harmonizes with the light within our Higher selves, it illuminates the darkened spaces of ourselves – the parts of ourselves we do not know yet (fears, broken and wounded places, dreams, angers, disappointments) and these hidden spaces seek light.

However, most of us presume the process of enlightenment (bringing in more light) as a mysterious, magical, ashram-sitting, "Ohming" into oblivion, magical adventure. Although it can have elements of this, a lot of the bringing in the light, in my experience, starts during

13

endarkenment and the exposure can be oh-so-messy, scary and often painful. For me, it has been more like cleaning out a dark, scary, stuff-I-no-longer-need closet, where everything comes out, gets spread out and generally makes a huge ol' mess all over the floor. But this is an on-purpose act (most likely from my soul's bidding – as our Feargo would NEVER allow such a mess!) and I get to:

1. Reveal it
2. Feel it
3. Deal with it
4. Heal it!

(Reveal, feel, deal and heal!) Notice that although it rhymes, "conceal" is not part of the process!

Yet, the dark sides of our being allow us the opportunity to reflect upon the light within. It is in knowing the opposite that we know the essence. Yet seeing that which is dark can be scary, daunting and sometimes feels as if we have done something wrong. But, the beautiful thing is that I realize when I turn around, the beautiful "light" is what is shining into the dark places of my life, exposing them so that in revealing them, I get to deal with them and finally heal them. So, the enlightenment (or "in"-Light) process is found in and through the dark.

When I turn towards the light, the shadows disappear. But, alas, I do have to turn around at some point to face difficulties head-on. But until I do, I can recognize that my soul will light the way, despite what my Feargo (fear) tells me!

As I learn to play with the light (and the dark), it becomes less scary.

Oh yea. Thank you, Divine!

Meditation:

Breathing in deeply, imagine a little ball of light in the middle of your forehead. Imagine that light growing bigger and bigger until it encompasses your entire being. As you feel the warmth of the light engulfing you, breathe in the comfort of the sweet Divine Love.

In This Sacred Place of Play Filled with Divine Love, Ask Yourself:

Where can I bring more light into the darkened places of my life?

Can I be at peace just knowing that the dark does not mean the absence of light – just that in this moment, it is obscured?

Lisa M. Smith, Ph.D.

Swinging – Back & Forth

Do you ever drive to work and end up at work and you don't remember driving there? Or take a shower or put groceries away and when you are done, you don't *really* remember the experience? We often do things repeatedly in our lives without any real response because we have habituated what we are doing. Habituation is a decreased behavioral response to repeated stimuli…the more you see it or do it, the less responsive you are to it. Essentially, we are unaware of what we are doing. Sometimes we have moments like this. Sometimes we have entire days like this… or decades like this.

Play invites us into a world where we can be completely *aware*.

What if everything you did in your life was the same? *But* – how you experienced it was different? It's as if your black and white life is infused with Technicolor and because of that, everything comes alive for the first time.

So often we go through the motions of our life without the E-motions (*energy* in the emotion) behind our actions. I have caught myself going through the motions of life as I clean the house or take out the trash or shop or as I eat a scrumptious meal. The list can go on and on.

Wow – what would it be like to *really be there* and take it all in? We tend to take in the fun and escape the mundane (hence habituation). Yet, a good portion of our lives is lived *doing* the mundane. I want to live in such a way that I am not waiting for something to swing me up…I want to feel the swing up *and* down…don't you?

I recently had an opportunity for some time off when my daughter was with her Dad. I found myself struggling with this very concept. I was so tempted to just fill up my time with doing and more doing. It was

17

the old way of playing for me. So, although I made opportunities for "structured" play, I realized that I also needed time for unstructured play…time when doing "no-thing" would be considered doing something. In this time, I intuitively *knew* that something would just come forth if I was just patient and still and allowed the space for it.

Since I was struggling with this, I thought it would be helpful to share a little play pyramid I created (much like the food pyramid we grew up with). It is a way of re-framing and re-defining "play." Feel free to create your own – but this is what seemed to make sense for me.

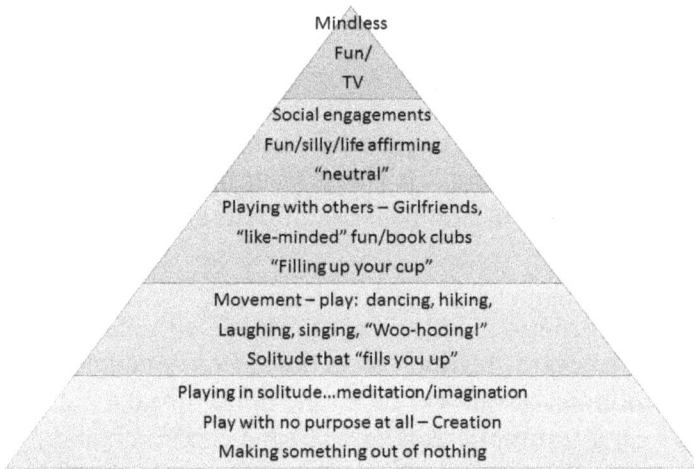

Mindless
Fun/
TV
Social engagements
Fun/silly/life affirming
"neutral"
Playing with others – Girlfriends,
"like-minded" fun/book clubs
"Filling up your cup"
Movement – play: dancing, hiking,
Laughing, singing, "Woo-hooing!"
Solitude that "fills you up"
Playing in solitude…meditation/imagination
Play with no purpose at all – Creation
Making something out of nothing

Meditation:

Take a deep breath. Imagine the space between your eyes and imagine that space filled completely with Divine Love. Imagine that space now growing and moving through your entire being. Sit with this feeling.

In This Sacred Place of Play Filled with Divine Love, Ask Yourself:

In what area of my life can I bring more play in (even if it is just in the way in which I do it)?

In the areas of my life that I consider to be mundane, is there a way that I can bring play to infuse this area with more joy (I have to do it anyway...why not?)?

Lisa M. Smith, Ph.D.

Ring-A-Round-The-Rosy

I felt like a tornado had just blown in and ripped apart my life. I felt raw, exposed, vulnerable and without a net. I felt as if things were collapsing and I had nothing to hold onto. I felt the fragility of my human self – a huge *not-knowing* and I was scared. I was also questioning everything I *thought* I knew. Maybe I had made up all these "answers" as some sort of safety valve. Although that was comforting for other people's problems…this was now about **me**. The problem wasn't *out there* – it was *in here* and it hurts, it scares me and it just plain sucks. When pain knocks on your door and tears sting your eyes, when your heart races in fear, your head feels light and the wind gets knocked out of you, all theories of life are thrown out the window. Sometime after, you have the choice to slowly begin to breathe again.

When you "get up" you realize you may have gone down, but you are not out. You still have air in your lungs and you breathe deep and you are slow to relinquish the tight grip that has been holding on to you.

It doesn't feel good, but it feels necessary – a propelling of your soul towards higher ground, but it feels like kissing dirt first. You just want to turn around and find out who pushed you. It doesn't feel like a choice but it doesn't exactly feel like you could be anywhere else either.

I now know why there's an eerie silence before a tornado. It's a brief reminder, a foreshadowing that the calm before the storm will carry you through to the other side where the peace washes over you. You may get relocated in the process but holding on to the center and standing in the eye (or the "I") of the tornado keeps you less likely to be tossed about.

The wind, rain and chaos will eventually stop. Your breathing will return to normal as you pick up the pieces and find shards of what once was you, shards that you may or may not choose to take into the future. But, more importantly, you have pulled together fragments of yourself in a way that would not have occurred had you not been pulled apart. Putting yourself together in a different way, giving you a new perspective, a sense of resilience and a new momentum for moving through to new places in your unexplored self. Pieces of ourselves strewn all over the place do not look so pretty, but we get through – somehow, someway, we are all able to continue despite our broken and fragmented selves. This leads us to reach a new wholeness – minus a few more holes.

To get from scared to sacred is merely the difference of two letters being re-arranged....but it is amazing how difficult the process is in arranging those two letters. Yet, it can be as simple as A-B-C – the "B" in between A & C represents "being" – just allowing and being with the emotion as it washes over us – the fear (which wasn't real to begin with....it merely "felt" real) passes through and the sacred is revealed.

We are spiritual beings having a human experience and through this human experience we get to taste our divine selves. Our human experience does not need to be negated so much as it needs to be negotiated. We get to recognize the Divine Love in the lesson. But, we can feel our way through to this as we fully embrace our experiences. We have created them on a soul level for our own growth.

Meditation:

Take a long, slow, deep breath. Feel parts of yourself opening up to be healed. Feel into the scared parts of yourself. Feel the breath seeping into all of the parts of you that have needed air for so long.

In This Sacred Place of Play Filled with Divine Love, Ask Yourself:

When my soul is relocating me to higher ground, can I rest in the "I" of the storm – which is my Divine Self?

Can I hold a space big enough for my soul to seep in AND still feel all that I need to feel on a human level?

Going to the Movies

I love going to the movies…it is a great place to suspend disbelief, step back and just observe. I love the feeling of just watching. No expectations of what will happen. You just take it in and experience it as it happens.

Through playing in and with my life, I have discovered that my own life is like a movie. Just like the movies that make me laugh, cry, that evoke anger, or compassion for those suffering, I am dreaming while awake, but all of it is created for me, and by me. When I view the actors I have cast in the roles I need to grow my soul, somehow they seem less threatening (and have less power over me – I have brought them into my life/play)! When I see that they are doing only what I have cast them to do, I begin to see a bigger picture of what my soul (which is the director) is trying to show me.

If I focus on the actors, or even the individual scenes, my Feargo (fear) can keep me distracted from the theme of the movie (which is to learn about love through my experiences – as love is the only thing that is real). If I can stay miserable enough by believing the thoughts Feargo by way of fear throws my way, maybe I'll miss the lesson that love would like to bring forth. Oh. Yea. That happens a lot!

So, as I grab the popcorn and settle into the seat in front of the screen of my life, I gain some perspective of the themes playing out in my life. I can then see all of the actors for who they are. They are loving soul-mates who have agreed to come into my life (and me into theirs) so that we can play out themes for each of us to learn. As the movie plays, I can imagine in some distant future, this person and I, who I seem to be really struggling with on-screen and who is evoking a massive amount of emotion from me as we play out scene after scene of seeming dysfunction, sitting after the making of the movie, laughing

Lisa M. Smith, Ph.D.

over a latte. We comment about, "Wow – that scene was intense...you really got into it. I almost believed you really thought that!" Or – "I think you're gonna get a Grammy for that role. Your role as a big asshole was awesome. You nailed it!"

Sitting in the seat allows me to take it all in and experience it, but bear witness to it without losing myself in the details of what is happening. I am a little more inclined to look for the lesson, to laugh when it's funny, cry when it's sad and get up and walk away when something has ended.

When the curtain closes, all I want to take with me is the lesson of love.

Wait. Maybe I want that now...Before the curtain closes.

Meditation:

As I take a deep breath, I see myself viewing my life from the seat of my soul. Sometimes I need to go behind the curtain to rearrange and redirect what is happening. Right here and right now, I breathe into this perfect moment and accept all that is.

In This Sacred Place of Play Filled with Divine Love, Ask Yourself:

Can I see my life from the space of love and what lessons my soul would like to teach me?

Am I willing to give up the notion that anything "out there" is doing this to me?

Am I willing to just watch, wait and see what happens?

London Bridge is Falling Down

Wow. Why did this game always feel so fun when we were kids? If you think about it, London Bridge (or any bridge for that matter) is falling down!? That's gonna be a mess and there will certainly be some carnage and wreckage from that. Ahh…we *played* with that concept as children because we inherently knew that life is filled with falling down moments. Why not play your way through?

After my divorce, the death of my father and filing for bankruptcy, I was trying to rebuild my life. I felt raw, exposed, vulnerable and without a net. I felt like I *was* the London Bridge as I was scattered in many pieces. The structure I had built my life around was crumbing and I was scrambling to grab at the pieces. All of the concepts that I had built my life around were smattering into a million pieces.

This certainly doesn't feel like *play*. But if play is an opportunity for me to try things on and learn and grow, why *isn't* this play? I think if I can learn that it is all part of a whole experience that I am co-creating with the Divine, then all of it is on purpose. I feel like I have learned that when I was finally able to gather the pieces together, I could examine each one individually as I put my life back together. There were some pieces that I recognized would no longer fit. Others had to be modified in order to fit the new picture of my life that I was creating. Some, well, they were just right and remained. But I realized that I would not have necessarily examined these things had I not co-created the falling down experience.

I began to realize that whether I choose to remodel my life on purpose (on a conscious level), or a gust of wind blows a hole right through the middle of my life (my soul taking over, because I'm not getting the message), either way, it is an opportunity to put pieces of myself back into *peace,* in myself.

Lisa M. Smith, Ph.D.

This is certainly worth falling down for.
"London Bridge is falling down, falling down, falling down.
London Bridge is falling down – (My fair lady becomes – My *Free*
lady)!"

Meditation:

As the tune to London Bridge fades into the background, take in a deep breath. Imagine areas in your life that you have perceived as having fallen down. Breathe into this feeling. Allow it to just be there as you watch the pieces fall. As you recognize that space that these fallen pieces have now created in your life, imagine those spaces to be filled up with Divine Love. Breathe that in.

In This Sacred Place of Play Filled with Divine Love, Ask Yourself:

Can I watch with no attachment or judgment as the pieces fall away?

Can I imagine a space of love filling in the holes that the pieces have created?

Can I take that love in – really take it in?

Merry-Go-Round

Do you remember the merry-go-rounds on the school playgrounds years ago? I remember in elementary school when we would all pile on the merry-go-round and get in the center and a few kids would grab the handles and run like crazy to make it spin around. I vividly remember the exhilarating feeling of sitting in the center and spinning. It was magical. At least back in the days when my vestibular system could tolerate so much centrifugal motion.

Why was spinning so much fun and natural as a child, yet as an adult it makes me want to hurl? Although there are physical reasons for this, I started to think about the mental, emotional, and spiritual reasons for this. As children, we are blank pieces of paper on which everyone leaves a mark. We learn so much, we are virtual sponges taking on the thoughts, feelings, and beliefs of all those around us.

Maybe as adults, we're just saturated. We just need a moment or two, to step off the merry-go-round and ground ourselves in *our* own thoughts, feelings, and beliefs. Perhaps we have to unwind and spin the other direction for a while so that we might let go of things that we "own" inherently, yet never gave our consent. I've done a lot of spinning in my life, where I take a problem that I'm having and spin it around the same petri dish in which the problem was created. Nothing new comes from that.

Perhaps it is time to step off the merry-go-round, drop to the ground and allow myself to unwind. I call this meditation. In this quiet space I connect with the Divine, my soul and find my center again.

As I learn to play in this space, yes, things may spin again. Sometimes I may spin with them. Sometimes I don't.

Lisa M. Smith, Ph.D.

Now, it's a conscious choice. Whee!

Meditation:

Take a deep breath. Imagine sitting in the center of a merry-go-round. Imagine that it is spinning and imagine that which you see is making it spin. As you breathe in deeper, your sacred self reaches out and stops the spinning. As you breathe even deeper, you feel the peace that comes from the stillness when you stop spinning.

In This Sacred Place of Play Filled with Divine Love, Ask Yourself:

Am I spinning without recognizing it?

What do I need to do to stop the spinning and just be still?

Am I willing to do that?

Walking on a Balance Beam

It is what it is. *It* is also *what it isn't*. Huh?

How can something be what it is not? Well, when it is daytime, it is definitely *not* night. No amount of wanting it to be night will make it so. Sometimes we define what something *is* by what it *isn't*.

I have learned a great deal about what I want by first learning what I do NOT want. This has been an interesting lesson in that my spiritual practice and exploration in the metaphysical world has groomed me to focus on what I want and how I can allow *that* to expand. But, how do you know if you really, super-duper, die-hard, never-want-to-have-anything-else love vanilla, if you have never tried another flavor? Furthermore, did you realize that there are many variations/flavors of vanilla?

In our oh-so-limited human form, we often lock down into what *is* and limit the endless possible variations in our lives because we are not open to what life has to teach us about what *isn't*.

Having been a single mom for over nine years now, I have dated intermittently and I learned so much about myself through this process. I learned more about what I *didn't* want, which helped me to clarify what I *did* want. However, I had to be open to letting go of the illusion of failure. I needed to have an acceptance of what was happening, (in spite of my expectations), and not attach myself to an outcome. These, of course, are beautiful theories in spiritual practice and believe me, I have collected a trillion quotes that have some facsimile of all of these theories. But, when it comes to living these Truths, well, that becomes a whole other thing. I guess that's why it's called a "practice." Ugh!

I have learned that everything not only has two sides, but a *whole* circumference of options available. There are a myriad of ways in which to experience something or someone. When I say, "It is what it is" – is that really true or is it just the way (or vantage point) I am viewing it at this place? What if I were open to what it isn't? What would that look like? Would a whole other experience spring forth from this space? Or what if…hold on – 'cuz this is about to get crazy… if "it is what it is" because it is exactly what *I* NEED (and on a soul level am drawing forth!)...what needs to happen in spite of my kicking and screaming? Ugh twice!

An example for me was being "let go" from a job. I had been hemming and hawing about leaving and felt in my oh-so-spiritual bliss that because no obvious answers (ok, what I really mean is "easy" answers) were springing forth, that the spiritually enlightened thing to do was to agree with my life and accept "what it is." Really, I was just scared to jump. So, I got pushed. Now, I could have said, "It is what it is." This person is releasing me from a job, that he admits I am phenomenal at. My department has improved exponentially and people love me (he says). What it could look like is a big freakin' mistake on his part…and on and on the Feargo goes. What it "is" is Spirit – nudging me onward. My GPS (God Positioning System) says, "When possible, make a legal U-turn!" What *it isn't* - is me being a victim/being fired. Although, my Feargo can (and did on occasion) make a very good case for this!

When we begin to circumnavigate our lives with the intention of seeing what *it is* and also what *it isn't*, we begin to get a clearer picture of *who* we really are. This makes for a very clear picture on how to move forward in our lives. It also makes for a peaceful and joyous ride!

…and so it is! ☺

Meditation:

With a deep breath imagine that you are looking into all that is (and isn't) currently in your life. With the intention of seeing that which you have not seen before, breathe deeper. As you take in an expansive breath, you also take in an expansive vantage point. You begin to see things differently.

In This Sacred Place of Play Filled with Divine Love, Ask Yourself:

What am I seeing differently?

How will this new perspective translate into a more peaceful, joy-filled, loving experience in my life?

Am I willing to see this differently?

Lisa M. Smith, Ph.D.

Uh...My Battery Is Dead

I lost my phone charger. It was an interesting experience as my phone battery began to lose its charge and I began shutting down programs that were running and then I shut the phone off altogether. I was in a remote area and I needed to preserve my battery until I could purchase a new charger.

It made me think of the correlation between the phone's battery and my own being. How many times do I get the "battery low – connect to charger" notice and simply hit the "ok" button and keep going? How many programs am I "tasking" on a daily basis that are taxing my battery and yet, I continue to let them run?

It seemed a good time to check and reconnect, literally and figuratively, with what charges me up. What practices do I have that keep me going and connected and am I consciously utilizing them and/or evaluating them for their effectiveness? Are there some software upgrades necessary?

Do I have things in my life that I just need to permanently delete?

I don't know about you, but sometimes I have way too many apps running. Oh, they are so interesting and fun and some are great time-savers (or so I tell myself), but how often am I really just simply plugging in and getting recharged? Sometimes, it is time to delete, reboot and engage the screen saver I call "my life". This is the stillness behind all of the other activities that surfaces when I cease the other activities.

Maybe it doesn't have to be a default setting.

Lisa M. Smith, Ph.D.

Maybe I can turn it on – on purpose. If not, maybe it's time to turn it all off and then plug in and allow the process of charging to take over until complete.

Meditation:

As you take a deep breath, imagine a space in the middle of your mind. Imagine that the screen saver of your life is one that emulates peace, love and joy. What does that look like for you? As you breathe deeper, imagine that screen saver taking over your entire being and bringing greater peace, love and joy to every cell of your body.

In This Sacred Place of Play Filled with Divine Love, Ask Yourself:

What apps (things) do I need to delete from my life because they are draining my battery?

How do I consciously plug in and recharge my batteries?

I Want a "Thumbs Up" Option for My Life

I love listening to music. But, I don't always enjoy the radio. I want to listen to the songs I enjoy, not listen to songs I have to tolerate to get to the songs that I enjoy. So, I began downloading music, but then I would get stuck in a rut and miss new songs when they came out.

Then…along comes Pandora. What a cool option – to design a radio station or stations that fit your personal interests and then have songs that are similar be gifted to you with the option of saying "thumbs up" or "thumbs down." I love this intuitive living thing.

I want this option for my life – don't you? Oh, wait. I think we do. When we attune (ahh…I love metaphoric language!) to what *is* and connect to the Divine Tuner, we can throw down our requests. Once we are vibrating at a particular frequency, "verses" (from the Universe! Hee hee) come our way that match our personal preference.

Now, we might have things that come our way that we don't prefer. We can "thumbs down" it by withdrawing our attention from it. Sometimes (I have the unpaid version, so I get commercials and only so many "thumbs down" options), we have to listen to a song we might not particularly care for. One of two things can happen:

1. We find an unexpected twist and actually *enjoy* the song, or
2. We don't like it anyway – but we can get through it. There's always the mute button!

However, as we begin to choose what we focus on and what we are grateful for, we "thumbs up" those. The "thumbs down" experiences become less frequent as we attune our will with the Divine Will (aka – the calling of our soul!).

The Divine plays along sending more and more a-tune-ment our way that we truly love. Then, in this Uni-verse, we truly are one verse!

Care to sing along?

Meditation:

Take in a deep breath and as you exhale, say the sound, "Ahh." As you inhale deeply, filling every cell of your body with love, repeat the sound, "Ahh." Allow this sound to echo in the middle of your forehead as you breathe and connect to the Divine Tuner. Imagine yourself being tuned by and in love.

In This Sacred Place of Play Filled with Divine Love, Ask Yourself:

Have I taken the time to acknowledge the things in my life I want to "thumbs up?"

Am I willing to evaluate those things in my life that could use a "thumbs down"?

Do I feel tuned into the vibration of the Uni-verse?

Treasure Hunt

A friend of mine showed me the book "7." It is a book about radical change. In the book, the author gives up 7 particular things for 7 months. Hmmm, I ponder - It is an intriguing thought as my friend and I discuss the possibility of doing this. She mentioned the first one – 7 foods only for 30 days. The whole idea is to recognize the ways in which we live incredibly abundantly and are not even aware of it or are appreciative of all that we have. Sounds like a great experiment. Then she told me the next one, which is wearing only 7 pieces of clothing for one month. I already felt my parasympathetic nervous system kicking in…my heart was racing, my palms were sweaty – air – I needed air. My reptilian brain sensed danger and it was ready to take action. Flee. Run. Danger. This oh-so-interesting spiritual experiment suddenly felt oh-so-incredibly threatening! ☺

Being an avid student of spiritual concepts, I have been in church and/or studied spirituality since I was in the nursery. There has never been a time that I can remember that I have not in some way, shape, or form contemplated God, the Divine, Spirit, Energy. I have looked at most religions at least once, read every spiritual book of intrigue I could get my hands on, sometimes reading several at once. I even studied metaphysics and received a doctorate in metaphysics and became a licensed ordained minister and metaphysician.

I have studied and have had an active prayer life since I was a young child and I have danced with meditation on and off for over 25 years. I still hover around, but it is a practice that I am willing to undertake as I feel the benefits are well worth it.

However, the concept of giving up something or things, intriguing as it may be, sounds like more work than 25 years of research, 2 sets of 48 exams and three 40 page papers. Funny, that was all about acquiring

Lisa M. Smith, Ph.D.

something…it seems to me that that would be a lot more work than giving up a few things!

As my breathing returned to normal, I knew I had to try this – or at least some facsimile of this, as it had brought up so much anxiety in me. What *was* this fear coming up? I had just watched the movie *Planet Earth* with Will Smith. In the movie, Will's character's son has to go retrieve an item on Earth that they had left behind because all of the animals on the planet had evolved to kill humans. His son was rightfully freaking out. Will Smith's character says to his son, "Fear is not real. The only place that fear can exist is in our thoughts of the future; it is a product of our imagination causing us to fear that which does not at present, and may not ever exist!" That is near insanity. Do not misunderstand me…danger is very real but *fear* is a choice…we are all telling ourselves a story!

I realized I was at a place in my spiritual journey that it was either going to become a story I lived or one I read about. Jumping in is my way of changing the story. It is my way of looking deeply into the eyes of fear, or what I have chosen to see as fear, and move past theory and into reality. I have no illusions that my giving something up in any way impacts the massive amount of poverty in this world. Nor do I think this small act of awareness in anyway can change the devastation of world hunger, of violence against the oppressed, the abused and neglected, the lack of drinkable water, and the list of atrocities goes on…

But, I do believe it will change me or at least the part of me that freaked out and maybe, just maybe, I can "let go" of more than just a few *things.*

Meditation:

As you take a deep breath, imagine the space of love that resides just beneath the surface of your skin. See this love expanding and enveloping you right now. Feel the love coming from you and coming to you all at once. Breathe it in. All the way in. See yourself centered in this fullness – a space where all that you need is provided.

In This Sacred Place of Play Filled with Divine Love, Ask Yourself:

When you think of giving something up, what is it that causes your heart to race the most?

Can you imagine why that is?

Is there any way you can explore giving it up – even for a little, just to take an objective look at the way Feargo is showing up and distracting you?

Lisa M. Smith, Ph.D.

I Spy

According to an old joke, *"How long 5 minutes is depends upon which side of the bathroom door you are on."*

Numbers are funny things, aren't they? They are truly autonomous – only signs based upon where the emphasis is placed. A high number, for example on a credit score is good. A high number on your cholesterol – not so much. A zero in your bank account - not good. Multiple zeros after a 1 in your bank account – very good!

It's all about context – what you see, and how you interpret what you see. A rainy day in sunny Arizona is a welcome reprieve from the harsh, blazing sun and is met with smiles by people – planning their movie-watching, snuggling-up-in-bed days. Rainy days in Ohio is met with canceled picnics, rained-out baseball games and possibly missed trips to amusement parks and that is met with disappointment and irritation. A snow day is a treat when you are a kid – you stay up half the night before a test praying for a snow day. As an adult, it makes life complicated as you contemplate how you are going to get to work in one piece.

What if life *really* was like this? What if we have duped ourselves into believing something is *bad* or even *good* when in fact – it just *is*. *We* are the ones who turn it into one or the other.

I recently watched the movie *Sliding Doors* and it was a very interesting movie where you were shown what would happen under two different scenarios. If the actress made a particular choice, things would go one way and if she made another, it would go a different way. It was a bird's eye view of seeing all of the things that coulda, woulda, shoulda happened. Yet, in the end – the life she intended *happened* – it just *happened* differently.

43

What if all of the "missed" opportunities, firings, rained-out days, losses and things we have labeled *bad* were just turn-arounds or ways in which we were redirected by our souls, before the off-track train collided and burst into flames.

Of course, it is impossible to perceive our lives from two differing vantage points but I wonder if we started with accepting what is happening, albeit not what was *planned* or maybe even *wanted*, as actually the better of the two scenarios? That the road traveled or *less traveled* is exactly the road we are meant to take.

I wonder how that might change how we view our lives. We still might get pissed off, disappointed and frustrated when we meet obstacles or experience loss or impasses, but we might stop long enough to think I am being rerouted on purpose. Like the all-knowing GPS that sends in another direction to keep us from experiencing delays or even potential danger, we are being spared.

We *will* arrive.

Or maybe we already have arrived.

It's all in how you look at it.

Or maybe – just maybe... the whole point is about the journey and being at peace, and "in-joying" the ride!

Meditation:

As you take in a deep breath, you are able to see exactly where you are in your life as being on purpose. As you breathe deeper into this knowing, you send out gratitude for the lost opportunities or missed experiences, knowing that you were spared and that your soul had other plans. As you breathe in the joy of exactly where you are at in this moment, you can see you are where you are meant to be.

In This Sacred Place of Play Filled with Divine Love, Ask Yourself:

As I view my life from a different vantage point, am I able to see all of the stops along the way that have led me here?

Can I understand that this place I am in is not only a destination from my past that I planned to be at right here and right now, but a starting point for my future?

Can I imagine that from here, I can go anywhere?

Lisa M. Smith, Ph.D.

Making Something Out of Nothing

Isn't it amazing as children we were able to create effortlessly and endlessly with very little available to us? I have watched my children seamlessly turn one object into another without missing a beat, simply because the "need" for it arose. The object of desire was not available, so voilà! They found something else to use. The process of creation is such an invigorating process.

To create is an inherent process. We are always creating. Sometimes we are not aware that we are creating (or from what we are creating). But we are always creating. Our thoughts, feelings and beliefs are the birthplaces of our creations. However, they can be anchored in Feargo or they can be anchored in love. Each one produces different results.

How do we figure out from which place we are creating?

To co-create in love is to play - with the Divine. When we do that the effect is more love.

> Love + Love = MORE LOVE!

> Fear (Feargo) + Anything = Still has fear (Feargo!) in it!

How do we empty ourselves of fear?

Maybe it is possible to start filling up with more love, while allowing the fear to seep out. Think about this… how darkness is expunged? You bring in more light.

You cannot shine darkness into a room. But you can shine light into darkness, which immediately dispels the darkness.

So maybe Feargo is not so much a thing as it is a *lack* of something –
much like darkness. When we wrestle with Feargo, it is like trying to
bring more darkness into a darkened room, while expecting to be able
to see.

Love is like X-ray vision in that it allows us to perceive things through
the darkness. But it does this by accepting that the darkness exists and
then slowly (like our physical eyes adjusting to lack of light) begins to
see "light" that we have not recognized before. We can facilitate this
process by asking a few questions:

1. Where is the love in this situation right now?
2. Where is the potential for *more* love in this situation right now?
3. How can I shift my internal perception to see that this situation
   holds only opportunities for greater love for me?
4. How do I open up – what do I need to do to receive the healing
   this love wants for me right now?

As we recognize that Feargo is only darkness – aka lack of light, it
makes us less afraid and more determined to find light. And the
greatest light in the universe is LOVE.

Meditation:

Take a deep, healing, cleansing breath. See a glowing ball of pink light in the middle of your mind. Feel that it is infused with love. See the love grow bigger and bigger until it is encompassing your entire being. Breathe in this love that wants to heal you throughout your entire being.

In This Sacred Place of Play Filled with Divine Love, Ask Yourself:

What situation am I dealing with that I could let more light/love in?

How can I see this differently, so that I am able to bring more light to this situation?

How might Feargo be keeping me in the dark?

Scared of the Dark

There is a quiet peaceful stillness in the morning, the dark space just before light erupts. It is the place I plunge into willingly, some days - shoved into other days. But, if I stop, breathe, and take in all that this sacred emptiness has to offer, I am filled up. Who knew that empty could feel so full?

I have spent many of my days here on this planet trying to fill up. Having been coupled since the age of 15, I don't recall having my own thoughts free from someone else's agenda for many years. I have spent days going to work, going to school, raising children, both with a partner and now, alone. Sitting with emptiness was not a feeling I was used to and certainly not one that I wanted to snuggle up with. I have spent nearly all of my life thus far, filling up the empty spaces.

Then one day I faced emptiness on so many levels – emptied of a relationship, a job, money and my house. I had been thrust into the darkness I had feared so much and at a level I had never known. I was scared of the dark and I feared there was not going to be anyone to come in and assuage my fears. I arose one morning and the darkness that engulfed me seemed unrelenting in its attack. It seemed as if there would never be any light. It seemed as if there never had been light to begin with. But, just as it does every morning, the sun began to peak through the darkness, illuminating the sky little by little.

As I began to surrender to the dark and scary places in my life, I began to illuminate this, albeit small, but powerful light. Just like the light breaking through the dawn, I knew not from where it came, but its luminous glow provided just enough light for that moment. The process of trusting that "enough light" would always shine, had begun. As I focused on what little light I could see, my eyes began to adjust so that my en-darkenment began to be illuminated into being in-light-

Lisa M. Smith, Ph.D.

moments. As I strung these moments together, a new dawn began for me.

I don't know if "fear of the dark" ever quite goes away. I guess that is the part of my *human being-ness* that I must simply acknowledge and accept. But as I turn my focus from the dark and toward the light, I am amazed and in awe of that which is illuminated.

I carry my nightlight within.

Meditation:

As you take a deep breath, allow your eyes to close slowly as you consciously see the light growing dim until total darkness is all you "see." As you recognize that this is an illusion of your own making, may this truth permeate all of the darkness within. Breathe into the darkness and see your own nightlight lit deep down inside. Breathe. Expand. Shine.

In This Sacred Place of Play Filled with Divine Love, Ask Yourself:

Can I be comfortable in the dark?

Do I recognize that the dark that I see is merely an illusion of the absence of light?

Can I find the gift in the dark – a space to turn on the light within?

Becoming Raw - I Mean Real

I was at the Desert Museum accompanying my daughter on a class field trip. The guide was talking about our Arizonian animals, their adaptability and survival mechanisms. The lady held up a sign that said, "Nothing in the desert *plans* to hurt you. They are merely protecting themselves." Wow. Human beings should wear a sign like that, I thought!

The presentation moved along through the desert animals and the presenter held a jar of shed snakeskin. The detail of the snake was intricately patterned on the skin and she told us that the skin came off in one piece but that the snake has to rub itself quite roughly for a very long time against a hard rock to release it.

It made me think of the past two years of my life and how the "skin" I was necessarily shedding of old thoughts, patterns, beliefs, and even people, had propelled me onto some pretty rough surfaces. It was purposeful scratching, much like the snake, in order to completely shed those things. I wish I could say that they came off in a beautifully patterned "one piece," however, my offerings were not quite so beautiful.

But, just like the snakeskin, it was merely a shell, patterned much like me, but no longer "fitting" the new me that I was becoming. The new, albeit raw, un-weathered, nor worn-in skin would take a little getting used to but I felt assured that just like the old discarded skin, this would serve the *new me* just right. I might need to scratch along hard rocks some time in the future, but for now, I get to stretch out upon the rock, relax and enjoy the warmth of the sun.

Lisa M. Smith, Ph.D.

Meditation:

Breathing in deeply, imagine the light of awareness, love and warmth coming into the top of your head. As you breathe deeper, imagine that it begins to permeate every cell in your body. Now, imagine that this light is washing over you and expelling anything no longer necessary to your being.

In This Sacred Place of Play Filled with Divine Love, Ask Yourself:

What might I be in need of shedding right now?

Are there any rocks that I am scratching up against that I can now see as necessary to the shedding process?

Where I might find sunlight during this process?

Finding Sunlight

Have you ever gone out to sit in the sun, found the perfect spot, sat down, turned your face toward the sun, relaxed, smiled, and took a deep breath only to have a cloud emerge and cover the sun? Sometimes it seems that life can do this to us. We position ourselves just right, or so we think, turn our face in the direction that seems right, only to feel blocked.

The difficulty is that maybe we don't know where to sit, which direction to face, and certainly, we cannot control the clouds. But in a moment of clarity, we stop, breathe, and realize this obscurity will pass because it always does. If I can just let go, enjoy the moment, accept and allow it, very soon, I will once again feel the warmth of the sun. The greatest news of all is that even in moments when I am not feeling the sun, it is still there.

But what about those clouds?

Growing up in Ohio I hated cloudy days. They seemed to be endless and carried with them a heaviness that was unshakeable. I felt swallowed up by a deep, dark sense of gray.

I moved to Arizona where the sun shines every day. Even when a few clouds roll in, the sun peeks out– even if only briefly each day. It tended to warm me from the inside out.

Then something weird happened to me. Over the course of twenty-five years of living in Arizona, having undergone some very stormy weather in my personal life, I felt a myriad of losses. They felt like tornadoes ripping through my life, stripping away so much of what I had held onto. But slowly I began to recognize the balance in it *all*.

Lisa M. Smith, Ph.D.

Granted, the sun with its warmth brings its gift naturally. Yet, too much of the sun can result in sunburn, heatstroke, dehydration, and people have actually died due to sun exposure.

Cloudy days bring coverage from the rays of the sun. Cloudy days can force you inside to do some much needed internal work. They can make you feel very disconnected from Source. But only if you believe that the *cloud* is the reality instead of the truth, which is that it is merely passing by.

I have learned to recognize the necessity of both the sun and the clouds in my life. For each of those things provide the vantage point necessary to keep my life in balance.

…and to be right here in the center. That's the sweet spot.

Meditation:

With a deep breath, imagine the warmth of the sun infusing your entire body with light. Now with that warmth inside of you, imagine a cloud passing by. Notice that it cannot affect the warmth that you have brought into your being.

In This Sacred Place of Play Filled with Divine Love, Ask Yourself:

What are the clouds that are passing by in my life?

Am I willing to see them as merely passing by?

Can I see the sun, just beyond the clouds?

Mom, Is It Warm Enough To Go Outside?

Growing up in Ohio, this was a valid question nearly every day of the year. I was a sunshine girl, even back then, so I was always seeking warmth. During the cold winter months I loved sitting next to the fireplace my dad had built. Later, he installed a wood-burning stove and I loved the nurturing warmth it engulfed me in. Now, living in Arizona, I appreciate air conditioning so much. Although I love the warm sun, 120 degrees, albeit dry, is still hot. It is truly a luxury to live in a day and age when we can mediate the temperature to our own comfort level.

I find it a perfect metaphor for living life as a spiritual being having a human experience. There is a certain temperature that just "is" whether we like it or not and we cannot control it whatsoever. We must adapt ourselves in order to live. Sometimes we may just have to be comfortable being uncomfortable. Then there is the space in which we live that we can adjust the temperature to our liking. Life can provide us with plenty of hot moments, when we feel we are being boiled alive. Although we cannot necessarily always change this temperature, we can adjust our internal thermostat by connecting with the Divine.

I have found living in Arizona that my body has adjusted to the heat. My tolerance has grown, so to speak. Now, 70 degrees feels chilly and I need a sweater. I feel our spiritual lives are very similar to this. As we get comfortable at one level (degree), we move to another. The Universe says, "Hey, you got this. Now, how about this!?" We are not being punished for our learning experience. We are just being given the next lesson in the course of the curriculum we have chosen to learn.

We are adjusting and transforming ourselves so that we can tolerate more and more.

Lisa M. Smith, Ph.D.

Meditation:

Take a deep breath. Imagine the space you are at right now. Imagine what the lesson might be in the curriculum you have chosen. As you breathe deeply into this awareness, wonder what might be the next lesson your soul is calling you toward.

In This Sacred Place of Play Filled with Divine Love, Ask Yourself:

Can I imagine the lesson this heating experience is trying to bring forth?

Can I imagine how my tolerance is growing?

Skipping Rope

I loved skipping rope as a child. It was a joyful activity to do alone and also with friends. Jumping rope is all about timing. You have to get into a rhythm of knowing when to go up and when to go down. You have control of the up…not so much of the down.

It's an interesting metaphor for life. As my friend, Christine says, "I am in charge of the *output*, but I have to let go of the *outcome*." I control the up, the Divine - the down.

All circumstances come to us as opportunities to change us or as *The Course in Miracles* says, "Lessons (in Love) we have opportunities to learn from". We just have to explore our relationship to that which we want to change. We tend to want to "force" an outcome and change something on the outside to alleviate that which we are feeling on the inside.

What happens if we just sit with what we are feeling? What if we allow what is making us uncomfortable to do what it has come to do – to change that which wants to be changed within us?

I don't know about you – but I'm not so good at just *being*. I am a Capricorn and I like to *do*. Sitting, waiting, being still, and allowing have not come natural to me. Having fought to get things in my life, I have also had to fight to keep them. I have used up a lot of energy trying to make something *be* what it wasn't.

Fighting gravity usually results in kissing a great deal of pavement.

As I have learned to just be still, accept, and allow things to come to me, I have been amazed at all that has transpired.

Lisa M. Smith, Ph.D.

Maybe it really doesn't have to be this difficult.
As I sit and relinquish that which is holding me down, I go *up* easily. I flow and float with the rhythm of life. I can close my eyes and feel it moving in and through me.

And sometimes….a song bursts from deep within and the little hum takes over.

And I sing out loud!

Meditation:

With a deep breath, sit in the stillness of the moment and imagine yourself as a child, skipping rope. Breathing with the natural rhythm of the up and down of the rope, see if a little song or hum doesn't come from deep within.

In This Sacred Place of Play Filled with Divine Love, Ask Yourself:

Can I be comfortable (as in – just notice) the uncomfortable?

What comes up for me in the stillness?

Dance Lessons

I love music and always love to feel the rhythm flowing through me. But many times I get out of step because I fail to hear the *real* music in my life as it gets drowned out by a cacophony of noise. Quieting my inner being allows the opportunity to listen to the inner music and once again get back in step and into the flow of my life. When I fight against the music in my life, I find myself to be in discord and disharmony and ultimately misstep.

I have never been a good dancer. It was not something I was allowed to or encouraged to do as a child. When I was eighteen, I went to see the movie *Footloose*. It changed my life. Not only was I in love with Kevin Bacon (and OK, who wasn't?), the story mirrored my own life. I grew up in a very small town and the religion I was raised with did not allow for Rock-n-roll or dancing. I was taught *not* to dance. I was told that the music I heard singing to me from my soul was wrong and to turn it off. I had acquired the coping tactics of generations before me. Silence the music. After seeing the movie, I literally could not stop myself from dancing on the sidewalk as we left the theatre. Something got switched on inside of me. The music blasted out from the depths of my soul. Little did I know that the music would hum me right into a new life. I would never be the same.

I think the movie appeals to a lot of people, because we can relate. We sense that somehow very deeply within us, there is a dance that is often squelched – mostly due to Feargo. This Feargo is fostered and then it festers. We start out dancing and fearless. Yet, along the way we acquire the fear based beliefs of others, which keep us from dancing our own dance.

Lisa M. Smith, Ph.D.

As I quieted my soul, stopped to *really* listen and feel my way through the magic of the rhythm, I began to sway to the music. As I listened even deeper, it began to take over and I started dancing with my life. When I fully surrendered to the dance, listened with my whole being and trusted that each step would always be there, my life *became* the dance.

Footloose and flying across the dance floor.

Meditation:

Turn on and tune into music that moves you (perhaps music from when you were a teen!) Take a deep breath. Close your eyes and allow the music to move through you and take over.

In This Sacred Place of Play Filled with Divine Love, Ask Yourself:

Is there any music deep within me that I have silenced?

Then be still and listen.

The Three Bears and a Little Girl

Trying to Find Her "Just Right"

As I get older, the fairy tales of my youth become more metaphysical and meaningful to me. I love the courage displayed by One Fair Goldilocks as she ventures innocently into a bear's home to find nourishment, support, and rest from her life. As a single mother, working fulltime (and being in school also) – I can SO relate to *that* pilgrimage.

I can only imagine what might have driven her deep into the woods. Perhaps it was a failed relationship, being let go from a job, an existential crisis or maybe just some much needed respite from the constant demands of being a fulltime Mom/Parent, breadwinner and student of life. That's a lot of "full" and maybe not enough empty. Maybe the lesson she needed to learn that called her deep into the woods was about finding some sort of balance in her over-full life.

For me, learning to lean into "Just right" and enough for now has been an ongoing ménage trois between too little, too much and just right. The Swedish word for it is "Lagom". The spiritual word is "The Tao." It is life lived in the middle.

I have often negotiated (or subjugated) my own needs for nourishment for those of others. My "porridge" intake often could be too much, yet leave me unfulfilled. Some days it was too little. Settling into *just right* has taken me some time (on both ends of not enough and too much) to figure out what that looks like for me. I have recognized that no matter how much is offered, it is *I* who has to take it in and decide. No one can do that for me. When looking for support, I realize that very often,

63

I reach for too much when it is not readily available. Conversely, I often accept too little support because I am not yet comfortable with receiving it. As I settle into just the right amount of support, I realize it is up to me to expand my capacity to receive before it will arrive. I recognize that within me, I must first have the courage to reach beyond just enough to just right, the wisdom to seek a balance of too much and just right and the receptivity to allow what is right for me to come to me.

There, with a satiated appetite, I can curl up in my "made for me" bed, pull up the covers and take a much needed breather after which I am ready to leave my little solace space in the woods and return to my life.

But I'll be back. As often as I need.

…and that is Just Right!

Meditation:

Take a deep breath. Play with your breathing. Take in too little. Then try to take in too much. Isn't it amazing that our bodies, in their infinite wisdom know what is exactly "just right" and that we are breathed without having to even think about it? Allow yourself to be breathed.

In This Sacred Place of Play Filled with Divine Love, Ask Yourself:

Is there something in my life that is just too much?

Is there something in my life that is too little?

Where might I be willing to find just right – right now?

Playdates with the Divine

Stormy Weather

Whenever I would have a breakup, I would watch the movie Twister. It fit perfectly with how I was feeling. For reasons far beyond me, sometimes I seemed to be chasing a storm that could possibly throw me around or relocate me at best and consume me at worst. In the movie, they explain the different ratings for tornados. An F4, they state will "relocate your house rather efficiently" whereas, an F5 is the "Finger of God."

I've felt both of those. It took me a few disruptions before I figured out that being tossed about was truly something I had control over. I didn't necessarily control the winds or debris, but I could grab onto something solid and not get whirled around too much. As I was able to accept what was being blown into (or out of) my life, if I remained grounded and held onto the center of my being, I was able to fly with the wind.

One of my favorite scenes in the movie is when the tornado chasers discover that they are about to be "eaten" by the tornado and begin running to find shelter. They find an old outhouse (appropriate in this analogy of relinquishing control and letting go, don't you think?) and they proceed by tying themselves to the pipes and hanging on. The outhouse structure is ripped to shreds. As the tornado passes over, they begin to float up into the center, the eye, of the tornado. There are a few moments of peaceful bliss and serenity as they are floating and the debris swirls around them yet they are completely safe and untouched by the storm.

I have found that when tossed about, I am forced to look at the loose ends in my life. Sometimes I have found myself snatching pieces of my scattered self out of the air and reclaiming them. Other times, I simply let them go. Yet when I strap on, hold on tight to the Truth of who I really am, I am unshakeable. I sit calmly and serenely in the "I" of my own storm.

Meditation:

Take a deep breath. Is life tossing you about? Are there things whirling around in your world that you are trying to make sense of? Breathe into the middle of your being and feel your core strengthened as the "I" – the truth of who you are.

In This Sacred Place of Play Filled with Divine Love, Ask Yourself:

Is there something that is whirling out of my life that I simple must relinquish?

Is there something or things that I need to just observe right now as I determine what purpose they serve (in loving non-attachment)?

Searching for Mr Right – As In Right Now

Writing a New Happily Ever After

I have spent most of my life in relationships or as I fondly named them, Rescue Missions. I started at age 15 searching for men in need of rescuing or fixing and tried to make them all right. (Of course, this was all judgment on my part…they were perfectly fine, on their own path, doing what they were guided to do by their own soul. My Feargo had decided to distract me by providing an erroneous belief that I needed to "rescue" them!

It was a masquerade for my own brokenness. I could hide my woundedness behind the Band-Aids of "the cause" of giving to another. I felt so self-righteous in my giving until I realized it was truly an act of selfishness. My unworthiness hid itself in the reflection of a man who came to rescue me, while I supported *his* dreams, or took care of the kids, fueled *his* endeavors and business while enabling *his* addiction. My lack of self-worth allowed me to lose myself in *his* disabilities, hoping to find grace *through* him.

Mr. Right had now become a mirror in which I had to see my own distorted reflection and face up to my own lack of clarity. When I stopped trying to fix everyone else, I saw myself and was able to move toward my own acceptance and healing.

Mr. Right became Mr. Right *now* and showed me how to become Ms. Right – and not for anyone other than me. I knew in my *Life Play*, I had cast all of these men to play the roles they did so that I might see myself through the mirrors they held up and to learn from these experiences. I finally gave to myself the love and attention that had been lavished upon others and found that *that* was Oh-So-Right!

As women, it's time to take back our happily ever after endings. We have been groomed as a society to prepare ourselves for that "One day when our Prince will come..." Yikes. What happens until then?

As I settle into the Right Now of my life, I realize this is the *only* Ever After I'll ever have. Here. Now. So it must be right.

I wouldn't have written it any other way.

Meditation:

Breathe into the Rightness of this very moment. Breathe into the Happily Ever After that your soul has created just for you. Breathe it into this moment. For this moment is the only moment you can ever truly experience. Right here. Right now. Breathe.

In This Sacred Place of Play Filled with Divine Love, Ask Yourself:

Can I be the "right" that I am seeking?

Can I be enough?

Can I be happy right here, right now?

Fenced In

I was sitting outside, meditating. I enjoyed the warm Arizona sun as it lit up my face. However, soon the sweet warmth turned into searing heat and it became too much. So, I turned around with my back to the sun and as the position of my chair would have it, I was facing a pool fence. From this perspective, it looked like prison bars. The irony was not lost on me as I reflected upon my current life. I felt fenced in.

Having faced many obstacles of late, I sometimes felt that my life had been turned round from the sun and it seemed that the shadows grew greater each day. I felt that if I could have turned myself around perhaps I would once again feel the sun. But for some reason, it didn't seem possible.

In this real life metaphor, I laughed at the ridiculous supposition. Of course I could turn myself around or I could even get up and walk away, for that matter. I pondered why the invisible bars in my internal life seemed so real and permanent. It seemed, from my limited view, which was all directed outward, that I was surrounded by prison bars with no escape. With this thought I intuitively closed my eyes and took a breath.

As I closed my eyes, so many thoughts and questions danced around on the landscape of my mind. What do I do? Where do I go? Why am I here? Hmm…it seems there were bars in there too. As I could feel the frustration rising within my body, I recognized that I had a choice at this moment. I could completely give in to the bars or I could just acknowledge their existence without any resistance, judgment or expectations.

So, I decided to just be with the bars. Even though they seemed to be of my own making, right now, they *feel* very real. So, as I continued *to*

Lisa M. Smith, Ph.D.

be with this feeling, I allowed myself to breathe. I acknowledge the thoughts and feelings but I recognized that I could also feel the warmth on my back just the same as when there were no bars.

…and then the clouds roll in. I'm like, "Seriously!?" I have just had this moment of pure "IN-LIGHT en ment" and now this cloud. Isn't that just like life? You go outside, find the perfect spot, sit down, turn your face toward the sun, relax, offer up a gratitude, smile and breathe and then a big 'ole cloud comes in and blocks the sun. Ugh!

Sometimes, we can do everything "right" yet the clouds still roll in. What then? As timing would have it, as I finish writing this sentence, the cloud moves away and once again the sun permeated my entire being. I laugh to myself as I think the Universe is playing with me (this *is* the theme of the book, after all!) and then I realize - it is dancing *for* me. Reminding me that what is real always remains. The sun will always shine on me whether there is a cloud covering it, whether it is obscured by the night sky, whether I am seeking it, feeling imprisoned away from it or when I simply don't feel like poking my head out to find it. It remains.

As constant as the Divine Love that it represents.

Meditation:

With a deep breath, imagine yourself in front of your own prison bars. What do they look like? Breathing deeper, what does it feel like to just see them, be with them and accept that real or not, they are of your own making? Breathing deeper, relax and see them dissipating.

In This Sacred Place of Play Filled with Divine Love, Ask Yourself:

What bars do I perceive in my life right now?

Might these bars be here to keep (protect) me from something?

Is there another way to perceive the bars in this moment that would be a greater sense of peace?

Sticky Messes

I sat down at my favorite spot to write and placed my stuff on the table to begin. I pulled everything out of my bag and got perfectly situated. Then, I noticed that I kept getting stuck in this sticky mess. I was all situated with no napkin in sight and didn't want to have to get up and haul everything with me to go find a napkin or wet wipe. So I continued to get sticky.

After about the third time, I intuitively just ripped out a piece of paper from my notebook to place over the sticky spot. I wondered why that hadn't occurred to me before. I think I was so focused on removing the sticky spot, I hadn't even thought of just dealing with it.

I realized how often my life can resemble this sticky spot. I know it's there. I am aware of how to fix it, yet I am not ready (or willing) to do anything about it. Yet, what was fascinating, is that although I "got stuck" a few times, another solution (other than the one I had first thought of but did not want to do) arose that both satisfied my desire to stay put and my need to not get sticky!

I pondered how this natural solution arose. It was in first accepting that there was a sticky spot and then still doing what I needed to do (as in – not getting stopped or distracted by it)! As I relaxed into what I was doing (putting my attention on what I wanted to do), a different solution snuck in the backdoor!

I am playing with the concept of no longer wanting any particular result or even setting an intention to create anything. I know – a radical concept huh? It seems almost counter-intuitive to what I have been taught. But it is something I am playing with. I ponder what it would be like to just show up to life and see what happens – sticky messes and all. I'm wondering when I have a particular concept in mind if I

73

don't limit the possible other options that might want to present themselves.

I don't know. But it seems worth pursuing. I am finding that when I am open to play with the Divine, I become aware of so many more possibilities.

I think I'll stick with it.

Meditation:

With a deep breath, imagine a golden light in the middle of your mind. See that ball of light growing and growing until it engulfs you in its embrace. As you breathe into this space, see yourself from all perspectives. Imagine that there are doors all around you as you stand in the center. Imagine yourself looking around at all of the doors – some of which you have never noticed before. Imagine that you are opening a new door.

In This Sacred Place of Play Filled with Divine Love, Ask Yourself:

What do I find behind this new door?

Are there other doors I would like to explore that I have been unaware of up until now?

Are there other possible solutions in my life to my perceived problems that I have not yet considered? Wait. Listen.

Playing Ball

I was watching the movie *Moneyball* and one of the players had a big fear of running to second base. He hits the ball and runs past first, falls and is scrambling to get back to first. Everyone is laughing at him and it is his worst nightmare coming true. But what he doesn't realize is that they are laughing because he has hit the ball 60' past the fence – a home run, and he doesn't even know it. He could have *crawled* to first base. He was too busy focused on and living out his fear that he took his eye off of the ball and suffered because of it.

I thought about how much this is just a great metaphor for our spiritual experience. We come into an experience locked and loaded with fears (good ole Feargo!) to work through and life can certainly facilitate their growth. Sometimes we get lost in the *reality* of our living situation. We are slipping and sliding around so much so, that we take our eye off of the ball.

What would it be like to experience *a knowing* that we had already knocked it out of the park? That the walk around the bases was a mere exercise and the homerun was guaranteed? How many of us have taken to the bench because we feel unprepared or we don't even know what position we are to play? Some of us are still in the locker room. It's ok. We are where we are because we need to be there.

I just wonder what it would feel like to get back in the game, to step up to bat and just see what happens.

Are we focused on the Feargo within us or is our eye on the ball of love deep within our being?

What would it take to get you back in the game?

Lisa M. Smith, Ph.D.

Cue…take me out to the ballpark!

Meditation:

Take a deep breath. Imagine your life as a baseball field. Where do you see yourself on the field of life? As you breathe into this space and meditate about where Feargo keeps you from stepping up to the plate, allow yourself to just breathe. Feel what comes up for you.

In This Sacred Place of Play Filled with Divine Love, Ask Yourself:

Am I focused on the ball of love that is within and all around me or am I distracted?

Am I truly stepping up to the plate I call my life or have I been on the sidelines far too long?

Flashlight Tag

Sometimes life can feel like a great big game of flashlight tag. You know – you are out in the dark, running around like crazy, looking for the light in others while shining your light intermittently, yet more often, hiding it from others so they don't find you. All the while – screaming – sometimes with delight, but a lot of the times from sheer terror – for when the lights go out, not only is it hard to *see*, things can seem quite frightening and downright threatening!

It would seem that since we come from nothing and return to nothing, that no-thing-ness wouldn't seem so scary. Why does it *feel* so terrifying to be lost in a sea of nothingness. We race around in our lives trying to fill the emptiness up with some-*things*: people, experiences, addictions, stuff, and more stuff.

What if our only sense of true inner peace and joy came from returning to that which we authentically are – no-thing? And what if, once we find this space we will truly feel at home? What if everything we have creatively designed in our lives – all the experiences, losses, ups, downs, and turn-rounds we have placed on our own path to bring us right to the very edge of no-thing-ness?

Yet, to actually *live* in the vast space of no-thing-ness in which all things are possible, we merely have to jump.

That's when it gets tricky.

This funny little thing called gravity trips us up every time.

Gravity (which comes from the same word that *grave* does), doesn't always feel so warm and fuzzy or something that beckons us to leap into.

Yet, leap our soul doth call us to do. *"Leap and the net will appear –
John Burroughs"* is one of my favorite quotes and one I learned to
live. This quote sounds great in theory. In practice, it felt like a WWW
smack-down. But, it was so necessary for my soul's growth!

When we are willing to surrender all of our some-things for the vast
no-thing space in and all around us, we might find what we have been
looking for all along.

Home.

And there's no place like home.

Heaven on Earth.

Meditation:

*Taking a deep breath, imagine yourself in the vast dark space of no-
thingness. It is less of an absence of presence and more of the presence
of absence. It is a palpable feeling that holds in it pure potential –
yours.*

In This Sacred Place of Play Filled with Divine Love, Ask Yourself:

Can I rest in the space of the unknown?

*Am I willing to allow myself to be still and wait for the answer to birth
itself from this vast space of the unknown (which my Feargo would call
nothingness)?*

Red Light, Green Light

Did you love playing this game as a child? Where someone stands at the end of the field yelling "red light" (which meant you had to stop) and then turned around quickly, yelling, "green light" to which you would scamper as quickly as you could without getting "stopped" to try and be the first one to tap them!

Ahh….good times.

Are you still playing this game for real?

What this might look like is always waiting for permission…aka the "green light" to live your life in the way you want to.

When we were young, we didn't need permission to play. It was authentically *who* we were. Our minds were always in creative mode, turning nothing into something, over and over again. We *were* endless possibilities and limitations were mere illusions, which we dramatically dismissed – usually with a cape on and a wave of the magic wand in our hand!

Somehow, as we grow up, we abandon our authentic selves and are taught to conform to the "red light"/"green light" systems of others. We are handed the rulebook and we sign on the dotted line, before we have even had the opportunity to read the rules. You know the "check here box" that indicates that you have read and clearly understand the rules, which we have neither read nor understood!

It's what we do.

Then one day, we wake up. We review the rulebook to see that there are things in fine print that we do not agree with. As a matter of fact, most of the rulebook is clearly someone else's idea of what life is about and usually this book has been passed on for generations with hardly any edits or updates.

But if we look very, very closely, we will see that there, in very fine print, just beneath the surface of our skin, is a very small clause that says, "If at any time, hitherto, the undersigned commits to wake up to the truth of who they are, they are no longer bound by the rules of this rulebook. Permission granted to make your own rules."

Thank God for loopholes.

"Green light" anyone?

Meditation:

Take a deep breath and imagine the space just behind your eyes. In this vast space where anything is possible, imagine that all of the agreements you have made with your soul lie here. As you breathe deeper, your soul reveals to you that which is just beyond what you have been able to see up until this moment.

In This Sacred Place of Play Filled with Divine Love, Ask Yourself:

What do I see?

What do I hear that my soul is trying to wake me up to?

Playing Dress-up

When I was six-years-old all I wanted for Christmas was red patent leather boots. I LOVED my boots and would spend hours with my red boots on, a towel on my head (to emulate my long, flowing hair) and a hairbrush in my hand for singing. The little wonderlust girl inside of me knew how to play in exuberance.

Somehow along the way, my hair was cut, the brush was tucked into a drawer and I outgrew my boots. The little girl was told to grow up, be responsible and leave behind her childish dreams.

As I work with children, I recognize that we really do have it all backwards. Children inherently know the truth about life, living and the openness by which they live is so inspiring.

We hesitate in our adult life to live so vulnerably – so openly. We have been taught how to close off feelings, our dreams, our passions – what we were born to do.

When did we stop playing dress-up and imagining all that we could be and start dressing down all of our passions and dreams? We've traded our dreams for the dramas in our lives and wonder why we feel so empty.

When faced with a decision, what would happen if you asked yourself, "What would the little Wonderlust Wildchild within me do"?

Yes, the logical part of our brain will tell us that of course, she was wild and free. She had no responsibilities, no children, no bills. She *could* dream.

That is true. But I don't think that's why we stop dreaming.

81

We have learned to be afraid.

When we are little we have silly fears like monsters under the bed. We intellectually know they don't exist, even a little child will recognize that they aren't real. But they are still afraid. It isn't their reality that keeps us frozen – it's our *belief* in them.

We may have grown up, but we are still running from the monsters under the bed. What we imagine to be real keeps us from exploring possibilities.

Who would you be without the monsters? What would you do? Where would you go?

What would your Wonderchild do?

I hear my red boots calling.

Meditation:

Breathe down into the core of the child in you who knows…that Wonderlust, Wonderchild who is still connected to their Divine Sacred and Playful self. Breathe. Listen. What do they wish to tell you?

In This Sacred Place of Play Filled with Divine Love, Ask Yourself:

What did I imagine was possible when I was a child?

How do I bring a bit of that back into my life?

Jumpin' in Puddles

Some things are best learned in the calm.

Others in the storm

Willa Cather

I always giggle inside watching children walking with their moms and dads either during rain or shortly thereafter. Hardly any child can resist the delicious invitation to jump into a puddle that beckons somewhere just beyond them. It's like a universal impulse.

It is certainly squelched by most parents. It is usually admonished and children are chastised for doing it. The child will after all, ruin their shoes or their clothes or God forbid, hold up today's agenda!

I think it frustrates us more than it does infuriate us. Who doesn't want to puddle-jump through life? Answering the magical impulse within and jumping in and getting all wet!? That is the richness that life is. After all, life is *not* a spectator sport.

What stops us from jumping in? Why are we so afraid of a little mess and avoid it at almost all costs?

Maybe our question shouldn't be, "What will happen if I do this?"

Maybe the question should be, "What will happen if I don't?"

Look back over the course of your life thus far. Are you more disappointed about the things that you have done that didn't work out, or the things that you haven't done?

What's your puddle?

83

Maybe it doesn't mean you are going to jump in and get wet. After all, who needs to ruin a perfectly amazing pair of shoes! Maybe it is just about acknowledging the puddle. Looking at it, sitting next to it, dipping your toes into it. (Shoes off, of course).

One thing I have learned is that somewhere in the middle of jumping in without thinking about the consequences (as a child…because we don't have to be responsible for the consequences – that's what parents are for!) and being a full-fledge hyper-vigilant responsible adult, is a balance.

There is a way to explore the miraculous, the wonder, and the puddles in life, without damaging our stilettos.

Integration. A little bit, at the right time, consistently can get you where you want to go. Even a compass, changed by one degree, will ultimately land you in a new direction.

There is a way. There is *always* a way. Where there is a will – there's a way. Where there is a *won't,* there's an excuse.

Toe-dip anyone?

Meditation:

Take a deep breath and tap into the part of yourself that remembers what it is like to jump into a freshly formed puddle. Feel the energy and sheer delight of the prospect. Let that feeling take over your entire being.

In This Sacred Place of Play Filled with Divine Love, Ask Yourself:

What puddle would I really love to jump into in my life?

What is holding me back?

Sandbox

How big is the "box" you create in? Who made the box? Are there any rules? What tools are in there? Are they your tools, or did someone else leave them behind for you to play with? Do you have access to water in your sandbox to create sand castles and mud pies? Where does the water come from? Is it endless?

On a recent trip to Maui with my 11-year-old daughter and 22-year-old son, we went to the beach every day. The Sandbox of the Divine. Wow…talk about an endless supply of both sand and water. On our first day there we loaded up at the store with supplies and my son bought a huge selection of sand toys. It was so fun to see the endless hours of fun as they created over and over.

One day the two of them were creating sand castles and were near completion when a huge wave came up and leveled their creations. My daughter, in her frustration "kicked" the wave in protest. My son, always the wise-old-soul didn't miss a beat…he retreated back further and began to build trenches in front of a new castle to capture the water and ensure its survival should another unexpected wave come.

It amused me to see the different reactions. Riley eventually rebuilt, but had to work through (albeit brief) the stages of grief first. I recognized myself in both of them. There are some losses that wash away and I simply retreat and rebuild. Others take a little or a lot more time and require a little kicking and screaming!

As I create, or in some cases re-create, I must ask myself, am I recreating the same thing and expecting different results? Am I entering the same job, relationship, or financial situation without having changed anything? Am I using old tools for a new situation? Do I have a Source that nourishes my creations and fuels my fluidity?

Life seems to provide endless opportunities for creation and re-creation. As a matter of fact, the word recreation (I.e., Play) is really RE-CREATION, as in creating again. Maybe the key to beginning anew, the re-creating, starts with play.

Maybe all we need is a bigger sandbox.

Or new tools.

Meditation:

Take a deep breath. Imagine you are sitting in the sand at the edge of your favorite beach. Hear the water as the wave crashes on the sand. As you breathe to the rhythm of the water, imagine the peace and joy being so near the ocean brings.

In This Sacred Place of Play Filled with Divine Love, Ask Yourself:

How is my sandbox? Do I have the right tools? Is it big enough?

What do I need to create in my sandbox right now?

Teeter Totter – Finding Balance

Zero on a number line is the exact center between negative and positive numbers. It is neither negative nor positive. It is the autonomous number. Having zero debt is good. Having zero monies - not-so-much. Zero is ambiguous. It all depends upon where it is placed.

To me, it represents a point of power in our lives. This is the place we can return to in order to find our center and the endless possibilities therein. It can represent infinite possibilities and with "no thing" in the middle it reminds me to keep my mind open to possibilities and clear of things that might knock me off center.

Life *does* have ups and downs. Why is that so difficult to accept? When we were kids going up and down was a thrill ride. I LOVED rollercoasters. Now, I want to hurl at just the thought of a rollercoaster.

Maybe it is because I have, metaphorically speaking of course, been on too many rollercoasters as of late.

What I have learned is that if I am able to step back (aka – find perspective), all-in-all there is a balance of ups and downs. It's almost like I go up to pick the fruit off of the tree but I also have to go down to tend the roots of my tree if isn't bearing any fruit. In some crazy-kinda-way, it is making sense. I read a metaphor stating that if you're going to re-wire the attic in your home you're going to have to go down into the basement to turn off the power first. When the job is complete you need to turn the power back on.

This is what I have experienced in the ups and downs. I go up to find a new way of thinking and I come down to integrate it into my will – into my human-being-ness. For example, I may want to be more

89

patient in my life. So I study, meditate, and seek higher wisdom and understanding of the concept (going up). But, ultimately, I must integrate what I have learned into my experience (going down). This "going down" might look like having plenty of opportunities and experiences where I get to practice my new-found-yet-to-be-integrated patience. This usually involves just learning to wait.

As we become more comfortable with going up *and* going down, we tend to find balance. This is a place where we can comfortably live.

It's a place where nothing can tip us over!

Meditation:

As you breathe envision yourself on a teeter-totter, going up and down. Imagine as you go up, you are breathing in and as you are going down, you are breathing out. Imagine that beautiful little space of quiet and nothingness at the top of going up and just before you go down. Linger there a bit.

In This Sacred Place of Play Filled with Divine Love, Ask Yourself:

What in my life makes me go up?

What in my life makes me go down?

How might I find my center? Listen.

Slide

Have you ever noticed the exhilarating feeling of sliding down is always precipitated by a climb to new heights? I observe children at the park going up and down the slide. Over and over again, they climb the necessary steps (which actually takes longer than the actual ride down), for the few moments of exhilaration as they *"whee"* their way down. It reminds me of being a kid in Ohio during the winter. We would bundle up to the point of near immobility, which would make the arduous climb even more cumbersome. Yet, we would do it over and over again. We would exhaust ourselves, freeze our buns off, get wind-chapped and wet, yet there was something magical about flying down the hill on the glistening snow that made it worth it – every single time!

I think of this now as I am climbing to yet another height in my life. Although I understand gravity (what goes up must come down), I guess in my spiritual life, I have a hard time accepting this reality. I like "up" or at least I feel in control of "up". It feels good. It makes sense and the daily, bothersome realities seem to fade – or at least the vantage point allows them to appear diminished. In my physical world, I know the climb up the slide will be worth it. I know I will undoubtedly get to experience the thrill of the ride, so I persevere. In my spiritual experience, I am uncertain of what lies at the top and even more unclear as to what the *letting go of* and the *giving into* experience will feel like. Will I lose my lunch? Will I have the courage necessary to do it? What if I fail or worse, what if I fall? What if no one is there to catch me? Wait. What if I succeed? What if I like it? What if it carries me somewhere else? Will my world change? Am I prepared to deal with this?

None of these thoughts go through your head when you are sliding down, do they? They only go through your head when you are climbing up.

How do we maintain the climb when the "whee" experience in which we are about to participate is uncertain?

Trust.

It is not that I don't understand, "it's not the destination, it's the journey". But, hey – I want to enjoy the destination, too. I'm not bundling up for nothing. The trust is not in some "out there" lesson that I will somehow acquire along the way. The trust is not in the hope that wherever I'm going it will bring me some sought-after happiness. The trust is not even in a benevolent Supreme Being "out there" to save me.

The trust comes in the willingness to surrender to the process of "bundling up," moving in the direction of what appears to be my "whee" experience, driven only by the sheer desire to move from where I am at. The trust comes in letting go of "down there" for "up there" without even knowing what *it* is.

The trust is in me. The part of me that knows and that has always known.

I *am* the "whee" experience expressing itself in physical form.

Everything else is just a detail.

WHEE!!!!

Meditation:

With a deep breath, imagine yourself climbing up a beautiful golden staircase. You are being guided by something beyond you as you climb. There is no real destination, only the innate impulse to climb upward. Breathe. Connect to that which is guiding you upward.

In This Sacred Place of Play Filled with Divine Love, Ask Yourself:

What does "up" look like and feel like to me?

When I envision going up the staircase, what do I envision myself headed towards?

What am I leaving behind?

Lisa M. Smith, Ph.D.

Monkey Bars

I recently visited my hometown and took my kids to my elementary school playground. I stepped onto the playground, and with the exception of newer equipment, everything looked the same as when I was there 40 years ago. I was struck by the dichotomy of how little things had changed there but how much *I* had changed – not only physically but also mentally and spiritually.

I grabbed onto the monkey bars and was hanging there for a moment and I recognized how the playground is such a rich learning ground, not only from a neurodevelopmental perspective, but also for life and things of the Divine. When we are children, we don't quite grasp how much freedom we have. We are so confined by the fences constructed by others that we have no perspective that what lies before us are endless possibilities. There are wide-open spaces just waiting for us to fill-up and create.

The Tao, *the way* of life is in the emptiness.

That moment just before something happens is filled with endless possibilities. Just before something pokes through the surface, we have no idea what it can or what it will be. It is the space, the silence before light and sound make their way to us that the endless possibility is all that there is. A block of wood can be anything in the moments before it is carved into something.

Why is it so hard to remain in this space of formlessness? It is almost in our limited capacity to take in all that could be, that we would often settle for anything – just to *know* what it is instead of waiting for the right and perfect form to take shape.

95

We do this by turning *not so right* and *perfect fit* people into partners, we turn jobs that are not right for us into careers, we turn material things into a substitute for real substance, and we turn food that is "food like" into nourishment. What we really long for is true connection, true love, deep meaning and purpose and effervescent joy. To turn a job into joy, we exchange two letters. We take out the "b" at the end, we ask ourselves "y" we are doing what we are doing and turn that into our "b"-eing. When we are being and living our purpose, we experience great joy.

I believe in our essence, we are longing for the freedom and peace of mind to allow all things to fall away and just be with the endless possibility of the unknown. It is very difficult to rest into that moment. The emptiness and trust that what comes out of the no-thing-ness won't consume us. To be made of *form* feels so strong, so sturdy and impervious. The illusion is that it is *real*. But the truth is, we are quite vulnerable in that we think what we don't know will consume us and eat us up. In fact, what really consumes us, are all of the things we use to fill up the empty space while waiting.

If we can just "hang" while moving from one bar to the next, while continually negotiating letting go of one thing and hanging onto another, I wonder where we might go? I wonder what we might find waiting for us on the other side of fear?

I wonder how much stronger we might become if we just let go of the bar we are holding onto and reach for the next.

Meditation:

Take a deep breath. Imagine yourself as a child hanging on the monkey bars. Imagine that feeling of letting go right before you grab onto the next bar. Imagine that this is not necessarily fear, but excitement. Excitement for the possibility of going exactly where your soul has intended to go.

In This Sacred Place of Play Filled with Divine Love, Ask Yourself:

What am I hanging on to right now that is keeping me from grabbing onto another bar?

Can I imagine just letting go and seeing what happens?

Trampoline

Gravity is a funny thing. Have you ever thought about it? We take for granted that we will not go hurling off into space whenever we leave our homes. Yet, stark reminders of gravity glare us in the face (or butt) when we look into the mirror at about age 40. Gravity has its ups and downs for sure!

It is a comforting thing but it can also be limiting – at least spiritually.

Jumping on a trampoline is an interesting experiment - especially after birthing several children. But it can allow us to experience a little more weightlessness than usual.

Have you ever thought about what things allow you to feel weightless? I certainly am astutely aware of the things that make me feel heavy – certain foods, music, TV shows – even people. They can certainly weigh me down. But do we take the time to concentrate on those things that boost us up? Do we take time to concentrate on those things that help us to soar to new heights and defy gravity altogether?

Sometimes my life feels very heavy. How about yours? Most days I skip merrily though my life as a single mother, without a true companion. I struggle with life's demands (bills, shared custody, grown children with their own struggles and a 12-year-old, changing hormones, sporadic income…blah, blah, blah). Somedays it feels like gravity has taken its toll and the sagginess and wrinkled despair is insurmountable and there is no "fix it" cream for it.

During these moments, my litany of levity creators seem to fall short of the gravitational pull of my emotions. The feelings, although I know that they will pass, seem to have taken up residence and no amount of negotiating will have any impact. What's a soul to do when the graveness of life pulls us down?

I'm trying something new. It's called surrender. Which is not the same as giving up. I've tried that too. I have given up many things in my life – some by choice, some not so much. But when I play with surrender, it is different. Surrender feels like a conscious giving up – a relinquishing to the fighting of the gravitational pull and just allowing myself to fall. It's like jumping up on the trampoline, and then allowing yourself to just be "caught" by the trampoline.

As I surrender this feeling, something interesting happens. I begin to feel lighter and that which was weighing me down seems to surrender itself too. In time, levity restores balance and I'm jumping up and down once again.

Meditation:

With a deep breath imagine yourself feeling lighter and lighter. As you continue to breathe in and out, imagine that you are floating – much like a feather in the wind. Imagine what it would feel like to just allow the wind to take you wherever it wanted. Breathe. Let go. Surrender.

In This Sacred Place of Play Filled with Divine Love, Ask Yourself:

In surrendering, can I imagine that letting go is really just an illusion as Feargo has convinced me that I must cling to this?

Can I imagine that there is peace on the other side of surrender?

Make Your Own Kind of Music

When we each came here, we *knew* how to dance. We would dance with music, without music – inherently. Most of us came pre-wired with our own music and our own steps. It seems as soon as we begin to understand gravity and we hit the ground running, we begin to set our rhythms to the Earth-bound movements. Here, although still connected by an invisible thread that moves in and through our being, we seem to all be awaiting an invitation to join the cosmic movement. While we wait, we adjust our own rhythms to those around us. It has become apparent that if we do not move with the tribe, it can be painful.

Just like any good lesson, sometimes we need to know and understand how something works, so that we can use it to work for ourselves. We understand it as it is, then we can break it down to work for our own individual tempo. This isn't always a comfortable process. There are many missteps and trip ups. The fluidity of our movement that carried us as children seems to be tempered by an indescribable heaviness of having to continually learn the steps of others and then unlearn them, to find ourselves still being tripped up by them.

I think the invitation to dance is our birthright and it is simply awaiting our acknowledgment of it. When we were little, it would call to us with such great passion, that many of us would fight sleep just to have one more moment of this delicious open space.

When did we stop dancing?

In our compartmentalized way of thinking, perhaps we believe that if we are playful, we are irresponsible. If we embrace the Peter Pan playful mentality, it must mean that we are immature and can't hold down a job. Maybe we started to truly believe all of the "have to's" that were thrust upon us and we forgot that we had a choice. When did

101

we lose our sense of wonder and our ability to fluidly move from "have to's" to "get to's".

I certainly have a continuously growing list of "have to's." As do you, I'm sure. I'm just wondering if we might be open to negotiating just a little more space for the "get to's". Maybe just a little space to see what is ours to do - differently. Maybe if we dance in and with gratitude, we can see it differently.

I may have found a secret passage door…it is through the hidden doorway of compassion. The root word, "com" is Latin and it means, *"coming together"*. Can I look without judgment and *with* compassion toward the part of myself that sees my life as a big "to do" list? Can I open the door a little wider to allow that space to grow into gratitude for all that is available to and for me? And in that space, can I nurture the possibility that, even though I began dying the moment I arrived here, I have come to live. To dance with life is to prove that I am alive. If I am able to see all that I get to do, maybe I'll find my footing once again.

Maestro, music please.

Your move.

Meditation:

Take a deep breath and listen to the music just beneath the surface of your skin. As you breathe ask yourself if you are still in harmony with its rhythm? As you breathe deeper allow yourself to sink deep into the movement of your soul.

In This Sacred Place of Play Filled with Divine Love, Ask Yourself:

Am I in step with the music of my soul?

Can I see my "have-to's" in a new light of gratitude, so I am filled with more joy, peace & love in my life – right now – just as it is?

Sticks and Stones May Break My Bones

But Names Will Never Leave Me

/ignore Button for Life

My daughter was telling me that someone was really frustrating her on Minecraft so she typed in the command, "/ignore" and their username. This way she was unable to "hear" what they were saying. Wow. I told her that I needed that option in my life.

But, even in the moment of speaking those words out loud, I realized that I *do* have that option. It's called Divine Love. It's my innate ability to see the love in whatever (or whomever) is presenting itself in my life at the time. It is really always my choice. I can either see through the lenses of Feargo or through the lenses of love. I'm not saying that is always easy or even where I go first. I just want to be aware that it is a choice.

In my experience, people give away what is inside of them. There were times when my children would tell me about the mean things the kids would say to them. As I listened and allowed my children to spill out their own bad feelings, we would talk about what must be inside the other child's mind to make them want to say such mean things. I would ask them what they got when they squeezed an orange. Orange juice, of course was the reply. I told them that we always get out what is inside – especially when "squeezed." And life sure does squeeze us, huh?

Why is it so difficult to *not* take what others say personally? What makes it so easy to take in another person's hurtful words when intrinsically we *know* it is *their* story – not *ours*. Yet, we take in the words, we are hurt or we build up anger and resentment from the words that are spoken to us. How do we heal it? How do we "/ignore" so that we can move on with our lives?

I've found that asking for the healing power of Divine Love to reveal the Truth of the person or situation has been helpful for me. When I am enrobed with the cloak of Love, I find that the words tend to be ignored and I am able to connect more with the *feelings* behind the words and the wounded one beyond the feelings. I begin to understand that hurt people tend to hurt other people. It seems the unconscious way in which we try to rid ourselves of our own pain.

I don't want to become unconscious with the person. That is not going to help either of us. There is another way. We can begin to "/ignore" the hurtful words while asking that Divine Love and Divine Wisdom unite in our relationships with those who spout their pain and to remove all resentment, the lack of forgiveness, and judgment so that love can flow freely.

Divine Love is like a free-flowing river between us. Although we remain our individual selves on either side of the river, sometimes we just need to remove a few boulders between us. Very often, we can even build a bridge from one side to the other and enjoy communion with one another!

This doesn't mean that we stay in relationships with people who continually say mean and hurtful things to us. It is *their* story and they need to go work out their own soul agreements. What I know is that if I am angry and if I hold resentment for another, I am *still* in a relationship with them, whether they are in my presence or not. I don't want to hold onto those feelings, for that is now affecting *my* story. In my experience, Divine Love neutralizes all of the "unreal" feelings (anger, resentment, hurt) and allows me to be free – truly free.

Meditation:

Feeling the Divine Love that is always available to us, take a deep breath. As you breathe in the healing power of Love, allow yourself to bring up anyone in your life that you have been "holding onto" – in anger & resentment.

In This Sacred Place of Play Filled with Divine Love, Ask Yourself:

Am I willing to allow Divine Love to neutralize this situation and this person right now?

What do I need to do to be free of this person and the feelings they bring up in me?

Do You Like Me – Circle Yes or No

I watched the Sex and the City series several times one year. After going through some particularly different break-ups, my Step-daughter bought them for me and said, "You need to watch these!" After having watched these shows a few times, I felt like I was becoming an expert on relationships – well at least the fictional ones. My *own* personal experiences had been somewhat less than "made-for-TV-ready!"

There are aspects of Carrie, Samantha, Miranda, and Charlotte in all of us. I found that I related mostly to Carrie and her on-going romance with "Big." If you haven't seen the show, in this relationship the series opens with Carrie meeting "Mr. Big" and the series ends (spoiler alert) with him finally growing up (and Carrie too) to self-love and recognizing *she was the one* all along. I could relate to her experience so much. I dated a guy for a while and I thought he was my "Big." He seemed larger than life in so many ways. Yet, it turned out that my image of him was my projection of what I *wanted* him to be and more importantly was what I was *afraid* to be myself. He was "Big" – but only in my mind. Granted, this wasn't his fault. I had disowned parts of myself and was happily projectile vomiting all over him.

But this provided some fertile ground for me to explore my own "Big" (and often seemingly small) self. I had to learn to say "No" (a word this disease-to-please girl had struggled with most of her life), set boundaries, but mostly open myself to receive a greater and deeper love. Sometimes even a whispered "no" to another can be a resounding "Yes!" to one's own self. I had this theory in reverse for many, many, (ok, all!) previous relationships.

I realized that I needed to drop my concept of a "Big" romance so that I could allow life's little lesson in loving myself to trickle into my

Lisa M. Smith, Ph.D.

heart and slowly expand it so that I could receive love in accordance with how I gave it. I had been asking others to give me what I had not given myself. The illusion I was buying into was that they had the magic key that unlocked the secret door to my receiving love and if they just unlocked it, I would be free.

Time and time again, the illusion was shattered. Yet, I somehow ended up feeling broken, more wounded, less worthy and less loveable. Because I mistakenly believed my value, worth and being unlovable was wrapped up in my giving; that if I gave enough, maybe, just maybe I would finally be loved.

I was half right. When I gave to *myself*, I opened the key to my locked heart. As I continually negotiated my concept of unconditional, equanimous love, I also learned to keep my heart open to receive. As I did this, I was able to see myself clearly and it is a love that is *Big* and it will never, ever leave!

Meditation:

Take a deep breath. Feel the love that you desire that might feel like it is outside of you. Feel it growing inside of you larger and larger with each breath. Imagine that this love is all there is and all that you will ever need. Feel into what that might feel like – to be complete without needing anything outside of you.

In This Sacred Place of Play Filled with Divine Love, Ask Yourself:

Can I be ok with just the love that I have for myself right here and right now?

If not, why not?

Can I see myself the way Divine Love sees me – as whole and perfect?

Living My Life As An Orgasm

Catchy title huh? Yea...the revelation that I had learned to live my life as an orgasm came well, uh during an orgasm. It culminated (pun intended) from a conversation that I had telling a guy friend what it takes for a woman to have an orgasm.

The truth is, no one can *talk* you to an orgasm. You can't *think* your way there. It's not a process. You actually *achieve* an orgasm by dropping out of your head and connecting with the feeling. You immerse yourself into the feeling until you have merged with it. You release all control of it, relax into the moment and simple allow it to come (ooh...this is fun) to you!

This is how I have learned to live my life as of late. Having been in school for the last eight years and finishing several degrees, I feel that I have had enough cerebral left brain thinking for a while. Certainly, in life we must utilize our brains and our ability to think and reason is such an incredible gift. Yet there have been many times in my own life when I *thought* myself right out of my feelings. I was left with no climax in my life – just a whole lot of work and erroneous and unhelpful thoughts!

Why is letting go and surrendering so difficult? The process of it seems so laborious, treacherous, and filled with festering fears. Yet, once we unclench our white-knuckle grip, peace, bordering on euphoria, can consume our entire being – leaving us breathless with the absolute sweetness that total and complete surrender brings. Perhaps in this human experience, we will always need to fight our way through this process.

But maybe, just maybe, if we become conscious of the deliciousness of sweet surrender and how *letting go* truly empties us to receive the

111

pulsating erect energy of the Universe, we might just succumb to it a little more quickly.

…and "O" what a feeling that is!

Meditation:

Ahh…breathe. Breathe into the parts of you that need new life and energy flowing into them. Imagine yourself relaxing deeply until you feel yourself held by this energy. Imagine yourself deeply open to the pleasure and release that this energy wants to bring to you.

In This Sacred Place of Play Filled with Divine Love, Ask Yourself:

Am I willing to live my life as an orgasm?

If not, what comes up for me when I think of letting go and surrendering to the delicious release that the Universe wants to bring me?

Blank Canvases

The sacred text, the Tao te Ching talks about *being* and *non-being*. It says we work with *being*, but *non-being* is what we use. In other words, we work with things in form (we can touch it, taste it, see it, hear it or smell it– it is tangible), but what we are using is the *non-beingness*. I have struggled with this concept for many years until I began observing children very closely. They totally get this concept. *Non-beingness* is that rich, ripe and expectant moment of endless possibilities. It is the blank canvas waiting to be splattered with creativity and the juiciness of life.

Everything that we know as *being* – those things that we end up holding in our hands has come from something, or to be more precise, from a no-thing-ness. Even ideas come from somewhere else and then are harnessed into form.

Where was the masterpiece painting before it was brought to life on a blank canvas? From what substance did the notes arrange themselves in perfect order to create a classic piece of music? This essence – the emptiness is the space from which all things come from.

Why is it so difficult to remain in this volatile space of formlessness? It is almost in our limited capacity to take in all that *could* be, that we would settle for just anything, just to *know* what it is instead of waiting for the perfect form to take shape.

What I think we are craving is the freedom and peace of mind to allow all things to fall away and snuggle into the moment of the endless possibility of the unknown. We want to be enrobed in a Divine Love that knows our very soul's longing and is committed to bringing that into the light. It just becomes very difficult to *rest* into that moment and the emptiness and trust that what comes out of the dark will not consume us.

Play is a process where we learn to move effortlessly from this empty space from which all things come from, into the space of living, where those things come into form. As we play, we learn to let go of expectations, surrender to what is coming into form and trust the process of co-creation with the Divine. Then, and only then, our soul's longings are coaxed out of the darkness, onto the blank canvas of our lives and transformed into a Masterpiece!

Meditation:

With a deep breath, look around the space you are in. See the many things that are in form. Imagine what was beyond that form before it came to be - the creative impulse that birthed the picture or the piece of music or the inspiration whispered to the artist that created the piece of furniture. Can you connect with that impulse?

In This Sacred Place of Play Filled with Divine Love, Ask Yourself:

What can I feel just beyond what I can see?

Can I see, or better yet, feel myself connected to that?

Sink or Float?

While designing a Homeschool program for a client, I was looking into many science experiments that fostered his interest. In so doing, we did a sink or float exercise where we tested random items to see if they would sink or float. While we were playing with this idea, we noticed that a large and heavy boat could float while a paperclip would sink. However, being a boy, he had to figure out how to sink the boat. All we had to do was keep adding water to it.

We talked about water displacement and how when we put an object into the water it displaces the water so that it can float. For example, when you get into the bathtub, you will notice that when you get in, the water level seems to rise. When, in fact it is merely moving to make room for you.

It is an interesting metaphor for life. Sometimes what is coming into your life is better than what is already there, so it must displace that which is there (which can feel like loss!) in order to bring this in. In my experience that which needs to be removed often goes first before that *new* thing comes in!

Sometimes displacement feels more like *you* are being moved instead of something moving to make room for you. It can feel like disruption. It can feel like a lost job, a lost relationship, or like financial difficulties. I have found that life just does that – it displaces us continually. There does not seem to be any magical formula to keep this from happening. I believe the magic is in our ability to figure out how to sink or float.

I started thinking that when I'm fully immersed in the water, there is more than enough water to cover my body. When I get out, there doesn't seem to be enough water. When I am "all in" in my life I am

Lisa M. Smith, Ph.D.

covered and there is enough. If I allow myself to just be held by the water of Divine Love, I can float – regardless of how choppy the waters are or how much water there is all around me.

Meditation:

Take a deep breath and imagine yourself floating in the middle of the ocean. Imagine that you are held there in the still, quiet and peaceful place of love. Imagine that this sense of peace and love permeates your entire being filling you with love and peace.

In This Sacred Place of Play Filled with Divine Love, Ask Yourself:

How can I let go and allow myself to be held?

Can I see myself connected to that?

Having All of Your Fur Rubbed Off

Real isn't how you are made, said the Skin Horse. It's a thing that happens to you. When a child loves you for a long, long time, not just to play with, but REALLY loves you, then you become Real.

Does it hurt?' asked the Rabbit.

Sometimes, said the Skin Horse, for he was always truthful. When you are Real you don't mind being hurt.

Does it happen all at once, like being wound up, he asked, or bit by bit?

It doesn't happen all at once, said the Skin Horse. You become. It takes a long time. That's why it doesn't happen often to people who break easily, or have sharp edges, or who have to be carefully kept. Generally, by the time you are Real, most of your hair has been loved off, and your eyes drop out and you get loose in the joints and very shabby. But these things don't matter at all, because once you are Real you can't be ugly, except to people who don't understand.

The Velveteen Rabbit

When I was young I learned that if you want people to love you, first – never tell them how you really think or especially how you feel and second, you are responsible to make them feel better.

So, I learned how to stop feeling (or at least shove those feelings *way* down) and unknowingly I was infected with the *disease-to-please* in an attempt to gain love and earn my keep in the, *you are worthy* world the adults around me had created.

I realize now that no one intentionally set out to teach me this. There were generations of unworthiness, unknowingly passed along as unconsciously as the bodacious hips and hazel eyes I had received.

Lisa M. Smith, Ph.D.

The concept of "not enough" was one my parents were painfully aware of, having grown up in severe poverty. It was certainly a reality they had to learn how to live through. It was a tainted heirloom passed down to and through them to me, merely because no other way had been known. It is difficult to ascertain what truly is a belief that you have fostered yourself, based on your own experiences, versus that which you call "mine", simply because it was handed down to you from others' beliefs and you have never examined it.

It has taken years for me to peel back the layers and question why I did what I did and when did it stop working (as if it worked at all – ever). Why did I continually give to those who had no intention (or perhaps even the capacity) to give back? They had become my surrogate father and I had made it my life's mission to MAKE them happy, win their approval and somehow redeem myself in the process.

Unbeknownst to me at the time, and as try as I might, happiness and worthiness is an inside job and certainly not one that could have been handed to me nor one that is earned through another person.

At the time, all I could do was well, "do" and do I did. To the point of exhaustion. It was an attempt to manipulate love, and thus validate my own worthiness.

But when you get down to the bare nakedness of your own inner worth and deep longings, you begin to withdrawal your efforts of love manipulation. Sometimes, it will require the rearrangement of relationships. Relationships are continuously negotiated and when you change the rules, others may or may not appreciate the *new you*. You may not have made them happy either, but you were making them dinner (or whatever it is you were *doing*) and they liked that arrangement.

They never asked you if you wanted anything. But why would they? I had never asked this of myself either. But once I did – a myriad of answers flooded my consciousness and the silence was broken.

Playdates with the Divine

It was the beginning of true authentic giving. First I learned to give to myself, to be open to receiving from others and then from a full and overflowing place, I could give. My cup overfloweth – what's in the cup is mine. What spills out is for you. In the end, trying to win my happiness and worthiness through someone else just didn't work.

I needed to go right to the source. Me. And the Divine Love that is continually available to me.

Meditation:

Take a deep breath. Feel the realness of love that is available to you right now. Breathe deeper into what that love wishes to make "real" for you right now.

In This Sacred Place of Play Filled with Divine Love, Ask Yourself:

Have I tried to "exchange" parts of myself for love?

Can I be open to allowing real love to come to me – without having to earn it in any way?

Lisa M. Smith, Ph.D.

Broken Pieces

My love vase (a beautiful red vase with the words "L-O-V-E" imprinted on it) fell from the counter and splintered into a million pieces. Picking up the pieces, the part that said "LOVE" remained intact. As I was throwing it away, my daughter remarked, "Mom, you are throwing *love* away." Hmm…I noted and then replied, "No. I am only throwing the broken pieces away because we could cut ourselves on them." As the words spilled from my lips I had to reflect on the obvious metaphor for my life right now. I had recently *thrown out* love – or what I had thought was love and I had been contemplating what love really was. Not like we all haven't done that a time or two, huh? I realized that just like the shattering of my vase, my illusions about what love looked like had been shattered. And just like the very small vase that had a limited capacity to hold flowers, my concept of love shattered, so that a new, expanded version could replace it. A new version that was ready and capable of holding more.

Things Break. The important lesson is in the willingness to sweep up the pieces and then throw them away. What the vase held (all the flowers and memories and even empty space) would always remain. I could hold onto the good parts but the jagged pieces would only serve to wound me. It was clearly time to let go of the pieces.

I haven't replaced my love vase. But I know that in time, another will arrive into my life, bringing with it the promise of more flowers, more memories and even bigger empty spaces to receive love. For in shattering the old, the new has already been created.

Just awaiting the opportunity to reveal itself and in this space of emptiness, I have found the greatest love. I have found love of my authentic self, which is way too big to be "contained" in anything! I love it when things break!

Lisa M. Smith, Ph.D.

Meditation:

Take a deep breath. Is there anything in your life right now that is shattering or has been shattered? Can you see what the falling-to-pieces might be wanting to bring into your life?

In This Sacred Place of Play Filled with Divine Love, Ask Yourself:

Is there something that has shattered that I am still trying to hold onto the shards of glass?

Can I be willing to let go of this with the openness that Divine Love wishes to bring me so much more?

Time Out

Sometimes in life you can experience what I call a "self-imposed, yet supported-by-the-Divine" Time Out.

Traditionally, we have interpreted a time out as a disciplinary action at its best and punishment at its worst. The *real* intention is to truly take some *time* out of life to regroup, to find your center and get your sh$@* together.

What it can *feel* like is punishment.

When I experience this, my first response is, "What did I do?" I have to kick that programming back to the curb because of course, it is my initial response. It is because of the beliefs that have been handed to me. When I step back to look at it, I can recognize the opportunity in this vacation from my life.

I wonder, what if this is the way (albeit different than expected and/or anticipated) the Divine is trying to support you right now? What if the Divine truly wants to play with you – in the space of silence and no-thingness? What if you are so busy *do-ing* ALL of the time, that the only way to get your attention (much like a wayward child does by pulling on our pant leg – when we aren't paying attention to them), is to call a Time Out?

I then have to look at my resistance to such a time. I declare my desire for a break, yet when one arrives, I resist it. What am I resisting in there?

I think it speaks to the fears that pop up when there is *no-thing-ness*. The ambiguity of the moment can be daunting, as I have no *tools* for not doing. I have amassed quite the collection of tools for doing...of that I am a master. Why is it that I struggle so much in the non-doing department?

It makes me uncomfortable.

I don't like to be uncomfortable.

Hmm…I suppose I shall get curious about that.

In a total space of not doing, not knowing and not supposing, I simply must rest. *Truly* rest in the Divine. I must trust life. I must have faith in love. I must simply allow the natural order of things without interference. It is what I meditate about. It is what I aspire to do.

It is just not what I "do".

Ugh. There it is.

Meditation:
Take a deep breath. Ponder what makes you uncomfortable. Is there anything you run from and stay "busy" so that you don't have to just be with it? What would happen if you just invited that uncomfortable space to come sit a while…I wonder what might come up.

In This Sacred Place of Play Filled with Divine Love, Ask Yourself:

Am I willing to bring in the uncomfortable and just allow it to be without doing anything about it?

Can I wait, watch and wonder as it provides an opportunity to know myself deeper?

Making a Wish

Aren't birthday parties fun? Do you remember the excitement you would feel as a child as your birthday drew near? There was a time for each of us when the *magic* of getting older was alive and palpable.

Remember that?

When did it change for you? When did your wishes turn into remembrances of years past?

Have you even stopped wishing altogether?

When did we lose the starry eyed wonder girl who believed in her soul that anything was possible? When did we stop believing?

I can't recall a specific moment. But I remember moments. I remember others telling me how much I could *not* do. That it wasn't possible. They would so eloquently point out the very round hole that my oh-so-squared-edgy self must fit into. They forgot to mention the pieces of yourself you would have to shave off in order to fit in.

But we do. I did. Because that is what is expected.

The resentment builds.

The frustration mounts.

Until one day – you've had enough. It might be a seemingly small and insignificant event that awakens the sleeping dragoness - or a life crisis. But make no mistake, when she wakes up – she is WIDE awake and there will be no going back to sleep.

The wishes she makes now come, not from some wimpy musings for hopeful outcomes. It comes from an ineffable strength, a faith in herself that she has been conjuring for a while. The magic she has been brewing has needed the time it has taken. It has needed the time to assimilate the ingredients and time for the heat to be applied to the ingredients to be able to work its magic.

Until she stands at the cauldron she calls *her life* and recognizes that the ingredients are all pieces of herself that have been sheared off throughout her lifetime. It has taken some time to get them all back. Some of them have not necessarily remained intact. But she's mending those. Some of them have been altered a bit. She is accepting of those. Some were necessary to let go. She has replaced them with authentic pieces that now serve her better. She has also even acquired some new pieces.

She stirs them together with the magic of a new found self-love and finds herself feeling complete, whole and loveable for the first time.

She feels no need to make wishes anymore for she recognizes the power from which wishes come.

…and it resides within her.

Meditation:

Breathing in deeply, feel the power that lies deep within your being – the Miracle of Self-Love that comes from your Soul – the part of you that is connected to Divine Love – that is in and all around you. Can you imagine this essence flooding your entire being with love and peace – right now?

In This Sacred Place of Play Filled with Divine Love, Ask Yourself:

As I stand at the cauldron of my life, can I see all of the pieces of myself as perfect and whole as they are?

Am I willing to love myself deeply and fully right here and right now?

Going, Uh ... #2

Stick with me on this one. I promise, I have a point! ☺

It is a reality we accept that when we let our literal shit go, it is gonna totally stink. There are entire industries designed to cover up, alleviate and distract you from this fact. But the reality is – it stinks. We find it uncomfortable to talk about this process. However, the reality is – if one is healthy, they will eliminate waste daily. In other words, if one were to hold onto waste that no longer serves them, they would become completely impacted and ultimately die.

Yes. I made this dramatic point for a reason. You probably know where I'm going with this.

Are we emotionally constipated? How often do we hold on to waste for way too long!

Now, I'm going to go out on a very long limb here, but sometimes we use our spiritual practices like *Febreze*, a product made to cover up and mask the symptoms and/or smells of our held-onto emotional debris. I really want to say *shit* here again…because that is oh-so-true – but I'll soften this delivery a bit!

On my meandering path of spirituality, I have acquired, let go and held onto many different tools, practices and beliefs along the way. There are so many that are helpful, encouraging and uplifting and I am so grateful for them. Meditation and prayer come to mind as prime examples of it. Radical acceptance, trust and unconditional love are others that authentically allow me to *let go*.

There are other tools that were helpful and meaningful at the time (much like training wheels or diapers). They supported me when I was unable to do so on my own.

There are some practices that become more like prisons and keep us from truly moving through and letting go of emotional waste. I frequently run into one common practice with my clients. For some reason, we have this incessant need to "Pollyanna" up our most painful and difficult of circumstances.

Now, before I go any further, I must confess. I am Pollyanna. I have played the glad game my whole life. I have always looked for the good and I generally almost always find it – eventually. What I have learned along the way though is that (now, stay with me here…) you cannot poop out food you haven't digested yet.

Yep. You heard me.

If you have not given yourself full permission to feel what you feel (i.e., digest your feelings) – you simply cannot release them and they stay in you – filling you with, uh… waste. And they keep you from moving on.

For most of us, this is simply a habit. We were either not heard or validated when we were children or worse, we were silenced and invalidated. So, not feeling what we really feel, is actually a more natural state for us than *feeling* what we actually feel. We were not given tools to move through it and process it. So, the one coping mechanism we had was to *not* feel.

But all of those unfelt (undigested) feelings are still there.

It's ok to feel. Feelings, like gas, pass. Yes, they may stink. Letting go of toxins can do that.

But wouldn't you rather have that stink outside of you and have it be gone, rather than linger inside?

So how do you go about digesting all of your feelings?

The remedy is:

Reveal
Feel
Deal
Heal

Reveal it – it's in there and most likely triggered by someone or something happening in your life right now.

Feel it. Where does it live inside of you? Can you identify a shape, or color or word or symbol to attach to it?

Now **Deal** with it. Once you have identified something you can deal with (it feels like a big black blob in the middle of my stomach, for example). Now take that big black blob visually out of your stomach and ask it what it needs or what it wants to tell you. Listen.

Now you get to **Heal** it. Cry. Scream. Draw. Run. Take a bath. Yell into the wind. Hug yourself. Let it move through you.

Do this as many times as you need to. Do it to completely release all that has been clogging up your life-force!

This is what it means to be free.

Oh yea!

Meditation:

Take a deep breath. Feel into your emotional digestive track. Is there anything in there clogging up your life-force? Breathe. Listen. Allow. See what wants to come up to be digested.

In This Sacred Place of Play Filled with Divine Love, Ask Yourself:

Even though I may have not been listened to or validated in the past, I am willing to listen to myself – right here and right now.

What is it that my Soul would like to say?

Sitting Still

Learning to meditate is essentially like learning a new language. It is the language of silence. Of being still. However, as a society in general, we are not so good at silence. It makes most of us extremely uncomfortable.

Look around. We continually fill up silence with music (listening to the radio and/or Pandora on the way to work), watching Netflix, searching the web, checking our Facebook status, checking Instagram and the list goes on and on. We have found and are continuously discovering more and more ways to fill up the silence.

I understand. Silence can be deafening. It can illuminate loneliness. It can scream out and expose the shadows of sadness, abandonment, rejection, and unworthiness that loom just beneath the cacophony of noise with which we fill our lives.

Siting with this can be extremely uncomfortable.

It can also be incredibly revealing and healing.

If we would just allow it.

Meditation is learning to create a background of silence. In doing so, we create peace and clarity in which to view the foreground as it plays out in front of our clear, present and peaceful background. This allows for precision-like responses to whatever is happening.

Lisa M. Smith, Ph.D.

It is simple.
It is not easy.

Our mind (Feargo) resists the idea of settling down and being still. It's ok.

Sit anyway.

Observe the "chasing of the tail" the mind does with detached humor. It is funny and it's quite a show when you don't believe everything you think. Eventually, just like the silly little puppy that chases his tail, your mind will settle down, even if for a moment… and just when you *think* it's not working, a little peace and clarity will sneak in.

And slowly, with continued practice, persistence and patience, stillness will envelop the noise in your life and peace will permeate your being.

When we become open to the offerings the silence wishes to bring to us, we are finally present to our own lives and that present is life's greatest gift.

To all of us.

Meditation:

With a deep breath, imagine a ball of light just above the top of your head. See that light growing and entering into the top of your head and slowly permeating your being. Imagine that as it comes in, the stress and concerns of your life dissipate – if only for a moment to make way for peace. Breathe into this space and see if you can expand it.

In This Sacred Place of Play Filled with Divine Love, Ask Yourself:

Am I willing to sit – if only for a moment each day to make room for the silence?

Am I willing to allow the silence to bring to me the gift of presence?

Playdates with the Divine

Having a Playdate

Being single – it can be tricky to meet someone. I have tried the Internet dating stuff and quite frankly – it is exhausting. A catalog of humans are presented to you – a slew of selfies (and don't even get me started about the half-naked-in-front-of-the-bathroom-mirror shots), which have been Photoshopped, along with stories about people's lives which are often half-truths at best. It is overwhelming and it feels like you are ordering a person through Amazon. *Primetime shipping anyone?*

However, you walk into a coffee shop, which seems like a respectable place to meet someone, and a host of single people with the hope of meeting someone themselves, linger there – on their computers and phones. Yet, no one approaches anyone, no one talks to one another. A sea of despair hovers just above the coffee smell, while lonely little islands wait for some magic gust of wind to blow them all together.

Why does it seem like we fail to connect anymore – I mean *really* connect?

Our conversations have been reduced to cryptic texts (many relationships have been ruined over misread messages – you *know* what I'm talking about), Snapchat moments and Facebook statuses.

How do we have an authentic meeting moment when it would seem that we have lost our authenticity?

We may have *selfied* ourselves into looking fabulous, but we have lost our *Selves* in the process. Just like many people do not look like their profile picture, many of us don't look like what we project to the world. We capture pictures, not moments. We're so busy cataloging the experiences of our lives, it is altogether possible that we have

137

stopped being *in* them. It is as if we are creating an autobiography of our lives – but not in retrospect – right while we're living (are we living them?) our lives.

How do we connect – really connect with another human being when we have lost our connection to ourselves?

Having an authentic playdate with another requires that we know and truly understand ourselves. It requires us to be willing to sit in stillness to find out *who* we are without the filters, the photos and without the "story" we project.

Can we strip away all of the theatrics and when we do, are we truly happy with who we are? Can we love the version of our True Selves that is not Photoshopped? Do we accept our beautiful, authentic without conditions?

When we are able to do this – to truly connect with *who* we are, finding our **Match** is a **Snap**!

That is a **Face** we want to **Book** a date with – for life! ☺

Meditation:

With a deep breath, think of the "Self" you present to the world. Breathing into this with no judgment, allow love to wash over you as you contemplate the real "Self" – the part of you that knows the truth of who you are and is connected to unconditional love and knowing that you are perfect – just the way you are.

In This Sacred Place of Play Filled with Divine Love, Ask Yourself:

Am I happy – truly happy with who I am without anything theatrics?

Can I be at peace and love the life I am living – not necessarily the life that I am recording for the world to see?

Riding the Carousel – WOAH! Horsey

Are you riding on a horse through the meadows of life with your hair flowing in the wind or are you barking orders to a horse that is firmly anchored to a carousel and you wonder why you keep spinning round and round – seeing the same thing over and over again?

What this might *look* like is a relationship with the same person – over and over again. Yes, they have different hair, different personalities and names, but they have the same issues – it's just a different date. It can also look like the same job – different company with different responsibilities – but same dead-end-stuck feeling.

We might try to drown out the monotony by distracting ourselves using social media, music, people, alcohol, food or shopping. But we still go round and round, still wondering why we aren't getting anywhere.

Eventually, the scenery gets old and we want to hit the pause button, tell that horse, WOAH! And get off!

W.O.A.H. –

Willing – first we must be willing to reveal inside ourselves what is keeping us stuck and we must be **willing** to deal with it. If I am constantly choosing a person (job, friends) that does not value me or treat me the way I deserve to be treated – am I willing to look at my part in this? Am I willing to look at the ways that I do not value myself and treat myself with respect? There is *nothing* outside of us that keeps us stuck. This is an inside job.

*I am **willing** to look inside for the answers that I seek.*

Lisa M. Smith, Ph.D.

Open – We must be willing to be **open**, willing to feel all of the feelings that have kept us stuck and we must be willing to heal those feelings. Sitting with uncomfortable and messy feelings can often leave us feeling vulnerable, exposed and powerless - much like the little child that was most likely wounded in this way many years ago.

However, we are *not* a children anymore and we have to remind ourselves that:

1) We do not have to repeat what wounded us in the first place –we need only to review it and
2) As we review it, we have our higher selves to guide us, protect us and comfort us as we feel and ultimately heal our wounded parts.

*I am **open** to feel and heal the wounded parts of myself.*

Accepting – We must be **accepting** of what answers come and we must be willing and open to receive something new. Sometimes this is the trickiest part. We have longed for something for so long and after we clear away everything that is in the way of receiving it, sometimes we have a difficult time recognizing the new and different. We then need to allow ourselves to receive it.

*I and willing & open to **accept** the new, the good and loving in my life!*

Happy – already. Nothing outside of us is going to complete us. As we become more willing, open and accepting, we recognize that our happiness is our *own* business and our own responsibility. We stop drowning ourselves in distractions and begin drenching ourselves in self-care and self-love and choosing to find (and make) our own Happy Place.

*I am willing, open and accepting that **Happiness** is my Divine right. I claim it now!*

When we finally stop spinning long enough to see where we would like to go so many other options open up for us.

Giddy-up horsey....I feel a no-rein ride coming up. Yee-ha!

Meditation:

With a deep breath imagine yourself on a carousel. Can you see yourself spinning round and round? Are there any areas of your life where this is true for you? Can you imagine that horse that you are on, just leaping off of the carousel? Can you imagine yourself flying free – with no reins?

In This Sacred Place of Play Filled with Divine Love, Ask Yourself:

Where do I see myself going when I fly free from the carousel I am on?

Am I willing to slow down the horsy – say "Woah!" and see what comes up?

Red Rover, Red Rover

Looking back at this game, I realize that this is a warped game and we wonder why we might struggle with self-worth as a society. Two lines are formed, people hold hands and call out the name of another person to run as fast as they can and try to break the bond that the others have created to keep you out. In other words, they ask you to join their "group" and then vehemently position themselves to keep you out. If the "called out one" is unsuccessful in breaking through, that person will be "captured" and will have to stay.

Wow. That's a lot of mixed messages in that game for a kid!

Why is it that we have such a difficult time breaking through in relationships? It's a wonder that we continue to try.

This has often been a metaphor for my relationships in the past. My name is "called" and I run holding nothing back, flinging myself into it, only to find myself captured and unable to navigate my way back out when I have determined that I need to do so. I have seen this with many of my female friends and clients as well. It is like there is an invisible link that is nearly unbreakable, regardless of the many ways in which we have been broken by the relationship. It seems impermeable and we wonder over and over again, why can't I break through this and why do I feel captured?

What is this and where does it exist within me so that I can extricate it from my life?

As I gain some perspective on my relationships of the past, I recognize that all of them have been created by me to see *me* – to **really** see myself from so many different angles. As I recognize the lessons of love that have been playing out for me and written by me, I begin to

Lisa M. Smith, Ph.D.

see my way out. These soul agreements really have nothing to do with the other person. They just hold up a mirror to reflect back to me. They show me where I am right now.

If I don't like the reflection, I get an opportunity to begin to change that which I do not like in the mirror. This, ironically has NOTHING to do with the mirror holder. Yes, the mirror holder may have to go. Especially when I change the reflection in the mirror and what they are showing me with their own behavior no longer resonates with the person I have become.

Our soul agreement has now been satisfied. Lesson learned.

Red Rover, Red Rover. It's over.

Time to move on.

Meditation:

As you take a deep breath, imagine a relationship that has been particularly challenging for you. Imagine the barriers that exist right now that keep you from moving on. As you breathe deeper, ask yourself what you need to move on.

In This Sacred Place of Play Filled with Divine Love, Ask Yourself:

How might I break through the limitations I have placed on myself?

What might the mirrors of my relationships be trying to reflect back to me?

Just Dance

My eleven-year-old daughter challenged me to a "dance off" on our *Wii Just Dance* game. Having seen two daughters successfully into adulthood, through the precarious waters of puberty, I knew the smooth sailing Riley and I have experienced thus far may be about to hit the open sea, with some choppy waters ahead. I accepted the challenge, although I have always had great insecurities when it comes to dancing! I knew I could be exposing myself to horrendous amounts of ridicule. But, I was ready – bring it on!

I found myself continually over-thinking the moves. The instructions and program lead you right through the moves. It really is quite simple, but I found myself constantly second-guessing my next move.

Finally, after about the third song, I gave into the inner-dancer and just let myself move without following the instructions. My score was the highest it had ever been. I even received a much-cherished compliment from my daughter. Maybe I shouldn't hang up my dancing shoes after all.

I thought about how life is so much like this dance experience. We spend most of our lives "learning the moves" as in following the choreography of others and second-guessing our own moves. But at some point, we stop *learning* to dance and we… *just dance!*

We first prepare to dance by learning the moves. It is also a necessary part of life. We must learn where to place our feet and sometimes this is a trial and error method, rather than having someone else teach us the steps. Sometimes we learn the steps from others.

As we learn how to find the music within us, we begin to practice our own moves. Sometimes we have a few missteps along the way.

Lisa M. Smith, Ph.D.

Practicing can often look like failure. But we are practicing and at some point, we'll know the steps by heart. And *life* becomes our dance floor.

But once we have learned the dance, we are ready for some fun. Now we get to play, explore and have fun with, not only the dance, but our inner dancer.

Then we are able to connect to the music and trust the Music Maker.

And then…you got it…we …

Just Dance!

Meditation:

Take a deep breath. Imagine your favorite song humming in the background. As you breathe and begin to sway to this inner music, allow yourself to just feel the music take over your body. Breathe and see how long you can just be in this space.

In This Sacred Place of Play Filled with Divine Love, Ask Yourself:

Can I hear the music calling me from somewhere beyond?

Am I willing to let go and just dance?

Filling Up a Backpack

Do unto others what you would have them do unto you

Luke 6:31

This is a great tenet to live by. However, the principle is often lost in translation. First, in order to *do unto others*, one has to be very clear of just *how* one wants to be treated. If you want someone to treat you in a particular way, you have to know what that *way* is going to look like. Then, and only then, can you reach out and *do* unto others.

We often get this turned around. We expect others *to do unto us* how we want to be treated, yet we aren't entirely sure of what that means to us. We have a very difficult time *asking* for that and then, we may have a difficult time being open to receive it. So, we end up *doing unto others* what they should be doing for themselves. We provide over-care in an attempt to fill up our inherent need to be loved, cherished and accepted.

We are groomed to do this. We are programmed to *be nice*, even when that means that we don't honor the truth inside of us.

As children, we are often silenced when we protest and are very rarely truly heard and validated. Big feelings can be incredibly difficult to deal with as a child and very few grown-ups have done their own work so that they are capable of holding a space big enough for such strong feelings.

Because of this, we end up carrying the weight of another's expectations, desires, and needs in our own proverbial backpack. We do not take time to evaluate how we truly want to be treated.

When we are able to set the backpack down and see who and what we are carrying, we might discover anger, disappointment, resentment, and frustration lingering in the bottom, like smashed crackers from a spilled out lunchbox in the bottom of a backpack. We know there is something down there, we just haven't taken the time or energy to spill it out and take a look.

Sometimes the clue in how we want to be treated can be found in how we treat others. What if we stopped doing for others what they need to do for themselves? What if we stop what we were doing for them and do the same for ourselves?

It's a novel idea. At first, this might feel very uncomfortable.

What if we were able to fill up the backpack of our lives with all that we desire and need and therefore we would not need anyone or anything to do that for us? This may look like saying "no" when needed. This may look like re-evaluating relationships that are imbalanced. This may look like self-care (massages, time-outs, time to meditate, hikes, bubble baths, etc.). This may look like stepping away when we actually want to step in and rescue. This may look like not constantly compromising and giving in to another's demands of our time, energy, and resources. This may look like asking for (and accepting) help.

Then, when we do give – it's not because we are trying to trade and get someone to reciprocate. We will merely be giving from a surplus of what we already have.

Then when we *do unto others* – it's because we've already given that to ourselves.

Meditation:

With a deep breath in, imagine yourself opening up to receive all that you desire. Imagine that your requests to the Universe for love, peace, joy, and abundance have been heard. Imagine as you breathe deeper that all of these things are coming easily to you now.

In This Sacred Place of Play Filled with Divine Love, Ask Yourself:

Am I doing unto others in an attempt to mask my unwillingness to do unto myself?

Am I willing to stop and examine what I would really like to receive?

Lisa M. Smith, Ph.D.

Climbing the Jungle Gym

Have you ever noticed that the higher you go, the greater your vantage point becomes? Do you remember as a kid trying to climb to the highest point of the jungle gym? It's like we knew that at the top... *that* is where the joy was!

When my son was five years old and we were trying to navigate our way through the challenges of an autism diagnosis, he was obsessed with tall buildings and elevators. We would always have to go to the top floor so that he could look out. It's as if he intrinsically knew that we would first of all, be climbing to new heights on this "adventure" and secondly, that we would need some higher perspective (in many ways) to do what we needed to do!

From the ground level, we are only able to see that which is right in front of us. It is hard to gain any perspective from this point. In our spiritual lives, the more aware we become and the more experiences we have, we are able to integrate those experiences as "knowing". As our "knowing" increases, we begin to *move up* throughout the rest of the "floors". As we go up (levitate), we must relinquish some of the heavier thoughts (gravity). Maybe that is the meaning of the term, en-lighten-ment as in "lighten" up. As one becomes free of the heavy thoughts, feelings and beliefs, which are so limiting, one's burden is lightened, making it easier to ascend.

From this point of view, we are able to make a little more sense of our experiences. Just like in a multi-level library, each floor provides its own set of books (wisdom, knowledge, and learning opportunities). Sometimes we can get stuck between floors as we transition from one level of awareness to another. The more we learn, assimilate and become aware, the greater is our ability to accept and trust the rhythm and perfection of a Universe that provides all of the curriculum

153

necessary to complete whatever courses we have signed up for in this "Earth School" experience.

It would certainly help to elucidate pain, poverty, illness, and some of the inexplicable happenings in our lives that can often feel overwhelming and all consuming. It is like viewing heavy traffic from the first floor. Our souls must have a level of awareness that our Feargos cannot simply comprehend and the higher we go, the clearer the view becomes.

Meditation:

Take in a deep breath. Imagine that you are floating upwards and are able to view your life from a higher perspective. As you breathe deeper into this experience, what is it that you see from this point of you?

In This Sacred Place of Play Filled with Divine Love, Ask Yourself:

What are the things at this point that I can see that pull me down?

What might I want to bring into my life that helps me to go up a floor or two?

What am I willing to see from a higher perspective?

Reading a Book

As one of us learns, we all learn. We are all one – a Sacred Unity – even if it doesn't feel this way. The more understanding we have of our inner-connectedness, the more we begin to see how very similar our experiences are. As each of us learns, we share this awareness with "the all." It's kind of like doing a book report in school. The class would all read different books and then we would share our learning with the rest of the class. This way, we got to learn from so many books, but only having read one.

It can be painful to watch the suffering of others through hunger, loss of a loved one, loss of a job, trauma, and illness. There are so many painful experiences in human form, much of which we inflict upon each other. War comes to mind here. Mother's children from one country go to fight and kill other Mother's children from another country. Yet, it seems that we resolve nothing doing this.

Yet we do it. Until we don't. Leaders like Mahatma Gandhi found ways of bringing about change without violence. Perhaps that evolves from one person reading and reporting back a different "book" than the book being "read" by the collective conscious at the time. Perhaps having heard hundreds of book reports of others, that seem to resonate the same, one person decides to seek out another perspective. In so doing, they bring that information back to the rest of us. Maybe this is how we may ultimately change our thoughts, feelings, and beliefs.

Even though we are one, we experience problems individually. Maybe this is the Universe's way of providing plenty of opportunities for a new perspective on the issue, thus it provides the possibility of a new solution to arise.

If *one* person can find peace amidst the turmoil, if *one* person can choose love in the face of hatred, if *one* person can reach out and offer help to the seemingly unworthy, then so can we *all*.

As one of us learns, we all learn.

If we are willing.

Meditation:

Take a deep breath and imagine all of us connected on a deep soul level. See that whatever it is that you are experiencing in your life, someone else is experiencing it as well. Imagine that this collective experience can open up a space for a collective resolution. One that brings more peace and love and joy to this time-space continuum.

In This Sacred Place of Play Filled with Divine Love, Ask Yourself:

Am I open to the experience of Oneness and the collective consciousness?

Can I see that as I go through what I am going through, so are we all?

Puzzle Pieces

Have you ever put a puzzle together and you get to the end and there's *one* piece missing? My eldest daughter used to "hide" a piece so that she could be the one to put in the last piece. I love doing puzzles. It is fun to scatter the pieces all over and then try to make some sense of the seemingly meaningless mess. Slowly, as you are able to fit the jagged edges together, a picture begins to form. It is so gratifying when you are able to complete it and see the whole picture!

Life feels a little like that doesn't it? It's as if we are given a big box of random pieces when we arrive here. We slowly open the box and pull the pieces out. It can often take a great deal of time to just turn the pieces over and imagine what it is you are trying to "make sense of". Sometimes it feels like you are missing a few pieces or that there are some pieces that just don't fit together. Sometimes, in frustration, we need to walk away from the puzzle and come back to it when we are clearer.

When going through situations that just don't seem to make sense to me, I try to take a breath, step back and realize one day this piece will fit in, make sense and a picture will begin to be clear.

In the meantime, I work with the pieces I have. I work with the pieces that *do* make sense and slowly, over time, as I assimilate all of them, I can see the picture begin to form!

And ultimately, the pieces turn into peace.

What a beautiful picture that makes!

Lisa M. Smith, Ph.D.

Meditation:

With a deep, cleansing breath - let go. Allow yourself to relax and in your mind's eye, look at the pieces of your life. Are there some pieces that don't make sense? Are there some pieces you are trying to fit in that just don't want to go in? Can you love yourself and breathe through it all?

In This Sacred Place of Play Filled with Divine Love, Ask Yourself:

Am I willing to look at all of the pieces in my life and accept that all of them belong to the picture I call my life, even if I don't understand how they fit?

Am I willing to accept the "missing" pieces (or what I perceive to be missing) as ones that either do not fit the picture of my life or are just not here yet?

Row, Row, Row Your Boat

It seems as a society, we are continuously adding things to our lives. We're *big* on portion sizes…Supersize -- want fries with that? There is a constant barrage of new apps, more memory or a new data plan for our phones…, or we can upgrade to the latest iPhone 4,5,6…We are often filling up before we even stop to see if we're already full. Obesity is no longer just a physical problem.

Sometimes, in an attempt to have a spiritual practice, we indulge (or over-indulge?) with books, mantras, affirmations, rocks, prayer beads, angel cards, oracle cards, candles, prayers, labyrinths, more books, more teachings. Yet, how often do we stop to ask, what might all of these things be trying to replace?

Why are we afraid to *feel* the genuine feeling of emptiness?

We very rarely feel authentic hunger pains. We are filling up before we even have any indication that we're hungry. Sometimes, we do not take the time to be empty enough to allow that emptiness to guide and direct us into that which would make us authentically full.

When we truly open up to what we're *really* hungry for, we find that it is substance and nourishment. These things generally don't come from a drive-thru window – spiritual or otherwise!

In our spiritual practice, we tend to add to what we already have in order to fill up the emptiness that the spiritual pangs of growth are creating. What would happen if we turned inward toward those pains and began to remove the obstacles to the truth of what we are really hungry for?

159

Maybe it's like being on a boat in the middle of the ocean that is sinking. In an attempt to save yourself, you throw out all that is in the boat only to discover that there is a hole in the boat. Once you plug up the hole, the boat stops sinking. You didn't really need to throw everything out, but in doing so, you discovered the real problem. You can now row around if you like and grab all of the things that you discarded that are now on the surface of the water. You can now decide what was truly necessary to begin with.

When we stop to ask what we really, really need, we also get to question, release, and heal all of the things we have held onto that are covering up the hole.

…And then we can truly row merrily down the stream!

Meditation:

Taking a deep breath, as the tune row, row, row your boat hums distantly in your head. Imagine the vast ocean and you in a little boat making your way wherever it is you are going. As you breathe deeper, imagine the things in your boat that you might want to remove. As you do that, do you discover any holes that are in need of repair?

In This Sacred Place of Play Filled with Divine Love, Ask Yourself:

As I evaluate my spiritual practices, am I looking to ensure that they have not become prisons?

Is there anything that I can throw out or just set aside for a bit, to determine if what I really need is just to connect – directly – without any tools to the Divine and feel the all-encompassing, healing power of the Love that is offered?

Capture the Flag

When I first began meditating, it became this blissful silence, a blissful escape. It almost became another world in which all of my fears, disappointments, failures, and pain would disappear. It was like Spiritual Prozac. There was a sense of calm and serene that would engulf my being. I didn't want to leave. Then, I would step back into life and I would feel so angry that my "outside" world didn't match my inside world. I kept asking, "Who stole my bliss!?" And of course, the Peaceful One inside, whispered, "you did." Ugh!

I realized in order to move through my life with greater ease, I would need to become clear about what was *out there* and what was *in here*.

In the children's game of "Capture the Flag", to surrender the flag means that you lost. Ah…how the Feargo doth reduce all things to either-or. You either lose or you win. Of course, the premise of the game is to chase after and capture the other team's flag. More chasing. More losing. It is easy to see how we associate surrender with something negative.

I have a far infrared sauna. In doing research on how it actually works, I discovered that the far infrared sauna will heat up the cells so that they spill out any disease and/or illness that reside within the cells.

Heat up. Yup. I've experienced this.

What it looks like can take on many forms: a lost job, lost income, lost relationships, losing my father, bankruptcy, losing my house…lots of "heat" has allowed me to spill out *lots* of thoughts, feelings, and beliefs that have been harbored deep within my being. I was unable to differentiate between that which was helping me and that which was

Lisa M. Smith, Ph.D.

hurting me. The heat allowed things that needed to surface to do so and then to be released.

Certainly it *did* feel like being consumed by fire at times. Surrender began to feel less like having my flag stolen and more like my handing it over to something greater that resided within me. Kind of like when you totally give yourself to the water in the ocean and you allow yourself to be suspended – half in and half out. There you are held.

Now, my life has become more like a meditation. I often sense no difference between *out there* and *in here.*

What comes, comes. What goes, goes.

I *am* the flag. Blowing in the wind.

I have never felt so free.

Meditation:

Take a deep breath. Imagine that within your being, beneath the surface are thoughts, feelings and beliefs that need to be released. Imagine that what might be taking place in your life right now is the "heat" necessary to bring these things to the surface.

In This Sacred Place of Play Filled with Divine Love, Ask Yourself:

Am I willing to be with whatever is happening in my life right now so that what wants to come up and spill out is able to do so?

Can I be at peace knowing that surrender is not giving up, but letting go of what no longer serves me?

Boo-Boos

As children, we inherently knew that to *immediately* release the feelings surrounding our pain was the greatest way to let go of them. Yet, often, the adults around us, unknowingly usually, would either move in too close to try to "fix" our big feelings, or worse, abandon us with our great big feelings, leaving us to try to handle them alone.

Sometimes, when we are experiencing great pain we just want someone who won't shrink in the sight of our not-so-pretty-and-oft-messy feelings. We want someone to be entirely present without feeling the slight bit of need to *do* anything.

Wow. What does that feel like?

When we sit with someone in great pain without doing anything, (truly – is there really anything we *could* do anyway?) it's like being a birthing coach. The woman in labor knows you are there, knows you can do nothing to help her – she must go through this alone, yet the fact that you are there provides comfort to her during the process.

When we can be comfortable in the silence and bring presence in this space, we bear witness in the silence, when words are not enough.

When we are able to do this for ourselves, we can provide the necessary space to heal. Big feelings require a big space and a big understanding and a big love. As the *now* grown-up, we can hold our little child's hand, sit with the big feelings (if we are willing to just be there) and allow those feelings to come up and move through us.

In working with children, I know that when big feelings come up, silence is the only element that will allow the *potential* of healing. Words tend to muddy the waters. However, we're not usually comfortable with silence, so we tend to try to rush in with words. If we are patient, the healing can arise – all by itself.

Then *we* get to be the one to give words to what we have been feeling and identify what we need.

Then comes the right antidote.

…Just wait for it.

Meditation:

As you breathe into the big space all around you, imagine that you are creating more space in which you can encompass all of your big feelings. As this space grows bigger with each breath, imagine yourself being held and suspended in this space.

In This Sacred Place of Play Filled with Divine Love, Ask Yourself:

Am I able to just rest in the silence and allow my feelings to bubble to the surface?

As I am held in this space, can I imagine myself healing all of these feelings?

Ashes, Ashes – We All Fall Down

Sometimes you win. Sometimes you lose. Sometimes you win – even *when* you lose. Games in which we attach meaning to winning and losing can leave one with the feeling that to "win" means to beat out the other. Someone inevitably feels bad - less than and left out.

How can this be deemed "winning" at all?

Trying to reconcile this on my spiritual path where we are all one, has been quite tricky. I get the concept that in *this* world, we attach meaning to winning and losing. Even young children get this. But, how can I feel good about my accomplishment when you feel badly about our experience together? How is that winning – for either of us?

What makes us divide in this way? What part of us thinks that this is not only acceptable, but preferred?

The part of us who knows by heart how to suffer –Feargo!

The further I step away from this part of me, the less I suffer.

The more, "I win" becomes, "we win" until even that falls away and all we are left with is, "we are one."

That is one win we can all cheer for!

Lisa M. Smith, Ph.D.

Meditation:

As you take a deep breath, imagine that we are all connected. In this space of connection, can you see that we are all experiencing much of the same lessons in love? Breathing deeper into this truth, feel your heart open to the Oneness.

In This Sacred Place of Play Filled with Divine Love, Ask Yourself:

As I am held in this space of Oneness, am I willing to drop some of the Feargo thoughts that keep me in competition with others?

When I drop these Feargo thoughts, what does Love open me up to?

Mother May I?

This is a classic game of asking permission to take "two steps forward". I remember it so well. I wonder when it stopped being a game for me and began to be the way in which I lived my life. Always asking for permission to move forward.

It's not that going backwards is so hard. It just felt so limiting. Yet, I have realized in going backwards on my spiritual journey that sometimes I have to retrace my steps for a couple of reasons. One, I discovered that maybe I had left something behind and now I have a new awareness around this particular issue that I can take back and provide some much needed clarity to. Two, I have often gone back to retrieve a part of myself that got lost in the experience.

As I was able to do this, I was energetically able to *review, reclaim,* and *renew* my resolve. As I am able to see things from a different vantage point, *review,* I am able to put together the shattered pieces of myself that had scattered, *reclaim,* and with this new awareness I could *renew* my belief in that which I had intended and set out to do.

Going backwards may feel like a delay or it may feel like we are repeating ourselves. But it is merely an illusion. We cannot go back to the same experience because we are not the same anymore. We are different. Life does that to us!

If you find yourself seeking permission to move forward, maybe it's time to go backwards for a few to see if there is anything back there worth reviewing.

Meditation:

As you breathe deeply into your being, see if there is any space inside of you that is still seeking permission to move forward? See if you can bring more light, love and peace to this space as you breathe.

In This Sacred Place of Play Filled with Divine Love, Ask Yourself:

Am I able to grant myself permission in this space of love to do whatever it is that my heart is beckoning me to do?

Am I able to let go of the concept that I need permission to fully play in and with my life?

Potty Training

Toilet seat covers. Great invention by a germaphobe. I love it. *Although* it has taken me years (since their creation) to figure out how to work them!

This has been my experience….I go into the restroom, grab one of these lovely little keep-my-butt-free-of-germs-covers, meticulously position in over the toilet, de-pant, begin to sit down and inevitably, the cover has now made its way into the toilet. Ugh. Really!?

I'm not sure why this idea has *just* now occurred to me, "Put the seat cover on just *right* before you sit down, Lisa!"

Brilliant.

I have been a planner my whole life. I like my ducks in a row. However, over the course of the past 10 years, the ducks were barely in the same pond – let alone a row. I had to learn to accept what was happening, when it was happening and the way in which it was happening. Ugh.

The seat cover was placed on the toilet seat, but only when it was needed. Not before.

I've learned that the Divine has always provided what was necessary in the moment. I stopped calculating. I stopped planning. I stopped being in resistance about what was *actually* happening.

The training was in me. It wasn't about making the world what I needed it to be. That is a massive undertaking in futility. It was about training myself. It was kind of like potty training. We don't "train" our kids. We train ourselves to stop and take our kids to the bathroom.

Lisa M. Smith, Ph.D.

I still grab the seat cover. It just makes sense.

I no longer fret about my coverage, though.

It is always just right!

Meditation:

As you take a deep breath, imagine the ways in which you are continuously planning, organizing and trying to control your life. Breathe into this space deeply and see yourself loosening this grip on your soul ever so slightly.

In This Sacred Place of Play Filled with Divine Love, Ask Yourself:

Am I willing to see the Divine in all that I do and relinquish the need to control it all?

Can I feel safe in the space of no thought, no planning, no "doing" and just BEING?

Telling Time

I have this beautiful wooden watch that I purchased for myself when I received my Master's Degree. It had taken a great deal of *time* to acquire this degree…with life-school being my study hall for quite some time. It felt like an appropriate reward for this effort!

It is beautiful and I really love it. It has two clocks and recently, one of the clocks, despite having the battery replaced, does not keep time. Well, that's not entirely true, it keeps its own time. It will randomly stop and then start.

I've decided to keep it that way. It reminds me so much of the *truth* about life. I have a clock that "keeps time" with the world…follows the rules, colors inside the lines, shows up on "time", because that is what we do, and what needs to happen for things to move in order and I acknowledge and accept this!

But then there is my clock that has gone rogue – the part of me that moves to its own sense of rhythm and occasionally stops to reset itself and starts again when it's ready. I am reminded that I get to move to the own internal tempo and schedule, too. Although the timing on the outside dictates certain things in my life, how I feel about it – that is an inside job.

Lisa M. Smith, Ph.D.

Meditation:

With a deep breath, imagine yourself in a space where time has no relevance. Can you breathe into a space where you are just free to be with no constraints. How long can you allow yourself to stay here? Breathe.

In This Sacred Place of Play Filled with Divine Love, Ask Yourself:

Has my life become a race against the clock?

Am I always running behind, or checking my watch or feeling as if I have no time?

Am I willing to see things differently?

Play gives children a chance to

practice what they are learning

Fred Rogers

So, as you head off to the playground of life, here are a few things I have discovered in observing children at play:

- They seem to have no fear or they are able to find strength and encouragement from peers – "you can do it!" **Find your tribe!**

- They are constantly making something out of nothing. **Create a space for *nothing* to come forth.**

- In general, if left alone they take turns and share. **Trust the Divine order of things and what is yours will always come to you – under grace and in perfect order!**

- They help one another…two can easily become one. **Don't be afraid to reach out for help and ask for it!**

- They can easily come together for a united cause – where strangers become friends. **Find those who resonate with that which you are becoming.**

- They change activities flawlessly. **Learn to be flexible, as perhaps the Divine wants to take you some place magical if only you'll go!**

- They are always giggling. **Find opportunities every day to reclaim and reconnect to your inner giggle!**

173

- They will do something over and over, and yet it is never the same thing twice. **Learn to see your life and the things you do differently. Put on your play goggles!**

- They have so much fun that they barely stop to eat/drink or pee. **When is the last time you had so much fun you barely stopped to eat?**

- They are boundless and are free to explore and discover. **Do you have healthy boundaries (both to keep out what no longer serves you and to let in that which you want to have more of in your life)?**

- They often lose the concept of time. **Can you get lost in timelessness where you can have, be or do anything?**

- The same boring sandwich eaten inside becomes magical outside. **Are you nurturing your innate self by spending time outside?**

So off to the playground of life we go. We will slide into life and dig for treasure in life's sandbox – ride the merry-go-round with giggles and glee and swing into new heights. We will seek the rhythm and balance while tottering through life's ups and downs.

Life is a playground....You cannot win if you don't play!

Play is training for the unexpected

Marc Bekoff

Lisa M. Smith, Ph.D.